Revelation

CATHERINE GUNSALUS GONZÁLEZ
JUSTO L. GONZÁLEZ

 Westminster John Knox Press
Louisville, Kentucky

Book design by Publishers' WorkGroup
Cover design by Drew Stevens

First edition
Published by Westminster John Knox Press
Louisville, Kentucky

This book is printed on acid-free paper that meets the American National Standards Institute Z39.48 standard. ∞

PRINTED IN THE UNITED STATES OF AMERICA

97 98 99 00 01 02 03 04 05 06 — 10 9 8 7 6 5 4 3 2 1

Library of Congress Cataloging-in-Publication Data

González, Catherine Gunsalus.
    Revelation / Catherine Gunsalus González and Justo L. González.
        p.   cm. — (Westminster Bible companion)
    Includes bibliographical references.
    ISBN 0–664–25587–6 (alk. paper)
    1. Bible. N. T. Revelation—Commentaries.   I. González, Justo L.
II. Title.   III. Series.
BS2825.3.G63   1997
228'. 07—dc21
                                                        96–49119

Contents

Series Foreword

This series of study guides to the Bible is offered to the church and more specifically to the laity. In daily devotions, in church school classes, and in listening to the preached word, individual Christians turn to the Bible for a sustaining word, a challenging word, and a sense of direction. The word that scripture brings may be highly personal as one deals with the demands and surprises, the joys and sorrows, of daily life. It also may have broader dimensions as people wrestle with moral and theological issues that involve us all. In every congregation and denomination, controversies arise that send ministry and laity alike back to the Word of God to find direction for dealing with difficult matters that confront us.

A significant number of lay women and men in the church also find themselves called to the service of teaching. Most of the time they will be teaching the Bible. In many churches, the primary sustained attention to the Bible and the discovery of its riches for our lives have come from the ongoing teaching of the Bible by persons who have not engaged in formal theological education. They have been willing, and often eager, to study the Bible in order to help others drink from its living water.

This volume is part of a series of books, the Westminster Bible Companion, intended to help the laity of the church read the Bible more clearly and intelligently. Whether such reading is for personal direction or for the teaching of others, the reader cannot avoid the difficulties of trying to understand these words from long ago. The scriptures are clear and clearly available to everyone as they call us to faith in the God who is revealed in Jesus Christ and as they offer to every human being the word of salvation. No companion volumes are necessary in order to hear such words truly. Yet every reader of scripture who pauses to ponder and think further about any text has questions that are not immediately answerable simply by reading the text of scripture. Such questions may be about historical and geographical details or about words that are obscure or so loaded with meaning that one cannot tell at a glance what is at stake. They may be about the fundamental meaning of a passage or about what connection a particular text might have to our contemporary world. Or a teacher preparing for a church school class may simply want to know: What should I say about this biblical passage when I have to teach it next Sunday? It is our hope that these volumes, written by teachers and pastors with long experience studying and teaching the Bible in the church, will help members of the church who want and need to study the Bible with their questions.

The New Revised Standard Version of the Bible is the basis for the interpretive comments that each author provides. The NRSV text is presented at the beginning of the discussion so that the reader may have at hand in a single volume both the scripture passage and the exposition of its meaning. In some instances, where inclusion of the entire passage is not necessary for understanding either the text or the interpreter's discussion, the presentation of the NRSV text may be abbreviated. Usually, the whole of the biblical text is given.

We hope this series will serve the community of faith, opening the Word of God to all the people, so that they may be sustained and guided by it.

Introduction

No other book in the Bible has been interpreted at cross purposes with the writer's original intent than the book of Revelation. Written originally as a word of comfort and hope, it has become for many a word of fear and despair. Written to bring clarity of insight to readers hard-pressed to make sense of their lives, it is now read as a gloomy and obfuscating book that can only be understood—if at all—by those holding the secret key to unlock its mysteries. Written to be read aloud in churches gathered for worship, its reading is now often reserved for sectarian conventicles and the ravings of fanatics. Hence the surprising paradox is that no book in the New Testament has inspired as many joyful and victorious hymns as has the book of Revelation, and no book in the New Testament has inspired as much destructive and even pathological behavior as has the book of Revelation. The reasons for these misinterpretations are many, as will become apparent in the course of this study. But at least two merit a word here.

First, we have lost the language. This is not to say that we can no longer translate accurately what the author says in his rather idiosyncratic Greek. That is not the problem. We have no major difficulty with the words themselves or with the grammar, and the NRSV, which serves as the basis of this study, is indeed an accurate translation. What we have lost are the myriad points of reference that John of Patmos and his readers had in common. It has been said that every verse of Revelation includes at least one reference to the Hebrew scriptures, and, indeed, some verses have several such references. John and his readers were steeped in the Old Testament and its imagery, so that words spontaneously and effortlessly brought about images and connections that we can only rediscover—if at all—through patient research.

Second, there are many references in the book to specific geographical, political, economic, and social circumstances with which John's readers were familiar. Although passing references were obvious to

1

them, we can only rediscover their meaning by way of a painstaking reconstruction of those circumstances. Even when, through patient research, we come to understand much of what John is saying to his reader, the very fact that we have to labor in order to understand his meaning makes it difficult for us to hear John's words with the same flowing understanding and emotional connections with which his first readers must have heard them.

This can easily be illustrated by means of the following example. Suppose that someone who knows English perfectly well, but who has little knowledge of English literature or American history, hears a politician say that he is about to tell "the tale of an ancient politician who one score and seven years ago a stately pleasure home decreed, a home which has now become an albatross hanging on his neck." How much of what has been said will that person understand? Certainly the words will be clear, if somewhat stilted. But the deep, cultural connections between the speaker and the hearers will be lost to anyone who does not know of Samuel Taylor Coleridge or of Abraham Lincoln. It certainly would be possible for such a person to come to understand what the speaker is saying and why, once each of the allusions is made clear. But still, the feeling and the reaction would not be the same, for the power of an allusion is precisely in its having no need of explanation.

This problem is quite clear to the writers of this book. We grew up in two different cultures, both of us living in homes that fostered a great love of literature, especially poetry. We can understand each other's language. Yet, we are painfully aware of how difficult it is to bring the other to the same level of appreciation that each of us has for the poetry and folklore with which each grew up. We can explain the words, the grammar, and the imagery; yet something is lost—much like a joke whose punch line has to be explained.

In order for the readers of Revelation to understand this book even more fully, we must seek to discover and to understand the references to the Hebrew scriptures and to the particular circumstances of that time. This is painstaking work, which in itself interrupts the reading of the book as it was intended to be read—out loud, as a flowing narrative, with unexpected turn of imagery and perspective. For that reason, we must also read the book in a different fashion: entire sections at a time, not worrying if there is a phrase or an image we do not understand, so as to recover something of the flow, rhythm, and emotion with which it must have been first written and read.

Therefore, as we write this book we ask the reader not to let the points that may remain obscure dim the luminous vision of Revelation itself. Try to understand as much as you can. If you keep trying, you will be surprised how much you do understand. And what you cannot quite understand, simply enjoy! After all, that is the way poetry must be read. And the book of Revelation, even though written in prose, has an unmistakable poetic quality. As M. Eugene Boring said, "not the least of the scandalous things about Revelation is that we ask for a diagram and get a mind-blowing picture; we ask for a logical explanation, and get a song" (Rogers and Jeter, *Preaching through the Apocalypse*, 77).

The odd reversal in the manner in which Revelation is read and understood says more about ourselves than about Revelation itself. In many ways, our situation as Christians today is the opposite of what it was for the Christians to whom John addressed his book. They were people with very little hope of success in the world. They lived in some of the richest cities of a mighty empire, yet they had no part in the power of that empire and very little part in its wealth. They were living either under persecution or under the threat of persecution. For most of us today, being Christian does not often pose challenges of life and death. We are fairly comfortable in the society in which we live. We have a stake in our society—in its positive values, as well as in some of its injustices. Therefore, a book that speaks of God's final judgment on the world, a book intended as a word of comfort and a promise of salvation for its original readers, sounds to us more like a threat or an announcement of doom, when so much that we cherish will pass.

Yet, we are not as far from the situation of the late first century as we might think. Although we may not face persecution, we face many situations in which we must decide between being faithful and being successful—or between being faithful and being popular. We are also part of a worldwide church that in many areas is living under circumstances similar to those of the first century. Injustice and idolatry are still rampant both in our society and throughout the world. For these reasons, it is good that the book of Revelation, with its dire warnings against those who would rather be comfortable or successful than faithful, is part of our New Testament. As we study it, we may discover that it has more to tell us than we expected.

THE AUTHOR

As you read the book of Revelation, you will find four places where the author refers to himself as John (1:1, 4, 9; 22:8). He never claims for himself any title except those of "servant" of Jesus Christ (1:1) and "your brother who share with you in Jesus the persecution and the kingdom and the patient endurance" (1:9). The only authority that he explicitly claims in his book is that he is "the one who heard and saw these things" (22:8). He may have been what was called a "prophet" in the early church—that is, one who speaks to the community in God's name (see 19:10 and 22:9). In any case, as we read the book it becomes obvious that he must have been a person of some standing in the communities to which he was writing.

Traditionally, interpreters supposed that the author of Revelation was the same author who wrote the Fourth Gospel—the Gospel of John. Most modern commentators, however, think that the style and cultural backgrounds of the two authors are so different as to preclude that possibility. Whereas the Fourth Gospel was written in rather polished—though still popular—Greek, Revelation was written by someone who obviously was more at home with Aramaic—the language commonly spoken in Palestine and which Jews at that time often called Hebrew.

As has already been said, the author of Revelation was well versed in the Hebrew scriptures, as well as in more recent Jewish traditions. His imagery is similar to the book of Daniel and to other more recent Jewish literature circulating at the time. His Greek is often awkward, like that of someone thinking in one language and writing in another. Furthermore, while all the other authors of the New Testament quoted the Old Testament in the common Greek translation that was then circulating among Hellenistic Jews—the translation known as the Septuagint—John either quotes from an entirely different translation or simply translates the passages from the Hebrew as he goes along.

All of this seems to indicate that he was a Jew—probably a Palestinian Jew—who had embraced the Christian faith. The traditions that ascribe to him the Fourth Gospel also say that he was John the apostle, the son of Zebedee. That is theoretically possible, and there is no way to disprove it, although this would make John a very old man when he wrote the book. Most modern authors consider this theory rather unlikely. In any case, it has little bearing on the meaning of the book or on how we interpret it.

THE FIRST READERS

John tells us that he was on the island of Patmos "because of the word of God and the testimony of Jesus" (1:9) when he had a vision, and received the command to write what he saw and to communicate it to seven churches in the Roman province of Asia (today, the western tip of

Turkey). As we comment on the text, we will learn more about each of these churches. In general, however, we can surmise that the majority of John's intended readers were Jewish converts, as he was. Otherwise, it is difficult to see how they could have understood his writing, which is so full of references to the Hebrew scriptures that only people profoundly immersed in the Jewish tradition would be able to understand them. As we read the book itself, we shall see that there was a debate, at least in some quarters, as to who were the "true Jews"—that is, the genuine heirs of the promises made to Abraham.

These Christians apparently were not in full accord as to how they should relate to the society around them. Some were more willing to compromise than others. In a society dominated by religious ritual, as most ancient societies were, Christians found themselves constantly faced with the need to make the decision whether or not to compromise their faith in order to gain economic and social advantage, and perhaps even to survive. If you made your living through a craft or a trade, you were forced to decide whether or not to join the appropriate guild. If you did not join, you would find your trade significantly restricted. If you did join, you would have to participate in their religious ceremonies, for guilds at that time were organized around the service and protection of a particular god.

In a similar manner, if you were a slave, your master would probably object to your Christian allegiance and also might expect you to accompany and serve him in various religious activities. If you were any sort of government employee, your position would require attendance at a number of pagan ceremonies. If you were a free woman, supposedly mistress of your own household, you would still have to accompany your husband in a number of his religious observances. No matter who you were, similar pressures would be constantly present.

In some of the churches to which Revelation was originally addressed, there were people who were quite willing to compromise in many of these matters. Others were not and paid dearly for their decisions—as was probably the case with Antipas in Pergamum (2:13). John himself was among those unwilling to compromise, for he was convinced that Christians should have no truck with idolatry. Therefore, part of the purpose of his book is to strengthen and comfort those who are suffering for their faithfulness to Christ and to chastise and call to repentance those who have compromised their faith.

It was traditionally supposed that when the book of Revelation was written, Christians were suffering a severe persecution under Emperor Domitian, who was often described as a megalomaniac who could not tolerate the refusal of Christians and Jews to worship him. Historians now doubt much of that traditional picture of Domitian, most of which has come to us through the writings of his detractors, all of whom served the next dynasty. Therefore, it probably is not accurate to think that the time during which John wrote Revelation was particularly bad for Christians or that John wrote in the midst of a general and cruel persecution.

Most likely, the actual situation was much more complicated. Christians who were willing to compromise and to participate in the common activities of society, even though this meant bending the rules against idolatry, apparently had no great difficulty with the government. However, those who sought to remain faithful in all things brought upon themselves the wrath of a government that could not understand such intransigence. From the perspective of those around them, they were subversive characters whose antisocial behavior must be punished. As for John, he fully expected that his call to greater faithfulness on the part of the church would lead to more persecution.

Several of the seven churches to which John addressed his book had been founded decades earlier. Some of their members were second- and even third-generation Christians. The initial fervor was beginning to subside, and compromise with the society around them seemed increasingly attractive. Should Christians remain forever marginalized from the economic enterprise when they could move ahead simply by joining a guild and participating in its worship? Couldn't those who had government posts keep them when all that was needed was a bit of religious flexibility? We can well imagine the debate in these churches, the dismay of some members when a brother or a sister succumbed to idolatry, and the joy of others when someone, at the cost of what seemed a minor compromise, was able to move ahead in society or up the economic ladder.

THE BOOK OF REVELATION

John was among those who felt that to compromise in these matters was to become guilty of idolatry. According to tradition, the reason he was in Patmos was that he had been exiled for his faith. His own words could be interpreted in that sense: "I, John, your brother who share with you in Jesus the persecution and the kingdom and the patient endurance, was on the island called Patmos because of the word of God and the testimony of Jesus" (1:9). His book clearly takes the side of those who would admit no compromise and calls them to faithful endurance to the end.

The very first word of the book in Greek is *apokalypsis*—revelation. This is not only the title of this particular book, but also serves as the name of an entire genre of literature that became quite common in Jewish circles in the last centuries before the Christian era and which Christians then took up and emulated. In general, apocalyptic literature seeks to deal with the suffering of the just at the hands of the unjust and does so in a highly symbolic language that combines liberal use of metaphor with numbers of often mysterious meaning. Since such literature generally is addressed to the faithful, it often speaks a language that is hard for the uninitiated to understand. Visions and their explanations play an important role in all apocalyptic literature and serve to explain why the just suffer, as well as to paint a picture of the final victory of God and God's chosen people.

All of this is true of John's *Apocalypse*, the book of Revelation. But Revelation has other characteristics that set it apart from the rest of apocalyptic literature. For one thing, while almost all apocalyptic literature is either anonymous or pseudonymous and places events in fictitious times and locations, often in the distant past (the other exception is another Christian book, the *Shepherd of Hermas*), John's Revelation clearly states its author and tells where he is at the time of writing. In this way, Revelation is more like the books of the ancient prophets—Isaiah, Jeremiah, Ezekiel, and the rest—who had visions and spoke in images and metaphors, but whose words clearly related to the context in which each prophet lived. And, perhaps more important, John's book differs from the majority of apocalyptic literature in that it has many of the traits of the epistolary genre. It begins with a salutation similar to other letters of the same period, includes seven letters to seven specific churches, and concludes the way an epistle would at the time.

Other significant features in John's book that are lacking in most other apocalypses are the constant references to worship in heaven and the frequent hymnodic passages. Through hymns inspired by it, Revelation has left a deep imprint on Christian worship, even though it does not include one word of instruction regarding how believers should worship—as do, for instance, the letters of Paul. In this, too, Revelation is almost unique in apocalyptic literature.

In brief, then, although Revelation has given its name to the entire apocalyptic genre, the book itself is different from the other extant writings of the same genre, to the point that one could even claim that the *Apocalypse* of John is not, strictly speaking, apocalyptic! (In the English language, according to *Webster's Dictionary*, one definition of the term "apocalyptic" is "foreboding imminent disaster or final doom." In this sense,

Revelation is "apocalyptic" only for those of us who, precisely because of our different circumstances, cannot read it with the sense of joy and comfort that was originally intended.)

There have been many theories proposed by various scholars as to the composition of the book. Some scholars claim that not all of the book was written by John, or even by a Christian. For instance, the theory has been proposed that most of the book comes from the circle of the disciples of John the Baptist and that the only Christian elements in it are the first three chapters and a few minor interpolations in other parts of the book (Ford, *Revelation*, 1). That theory, and many others like it, have not been generally accepted, and most scholars still believe that the book was originally written as a single piece—although quite possibly the author did use materials from other sources and from different times in his own life.

Whatever the case may be, such debates are not important for our purposes. To us, what is important is that this book, either as an entirely original writing or as an edited compilation, spoke the Word of God to its early Christian readers. These readers, in turn, preserved it and passed it on to ensuing generations who also heard the Word of God in it and thus included it in the canon (list of books) of the New Testament. Even more important, in this book we too shall find God's Word to us and for us.

THE DATE

Irenaeus, a Christian who was raised in Smyrna (one of John's "seven churches") and who wrote almost a century after the writing of Revelation, says that John wrote his book "near the end of Domitian's reign." Since Domitian reigned from A.D. 81 to 96, this would place the writing of the book around the year 95, which has been the traditional date. Writings from that era depicted Domitian as a cruel and almost demented persecutor, leaving us to surmise that it was in the midst of that persecution that John wrote his book.

The reevaluation of Domitian's reign and the probability that persecution during that period may not have been as fierce as previously thought have led some scholars to try to date Revelation either earlier—as early as the reign of Nero, in A.D. 64—or slightly later. Since none of these efforts have proven convincing, it seems best to let the traditional date stand, for—as we shall see in the course of this commentary—it helps us understand a number of references in the text of Revelation, and there are no real reasons to seek another date.

INTERPRETATIONS

No book in the Bible has been the object of as many, or as different, interpretations as has been the book of Revelation. By far the most popular interpretations—and the most widespread in our day—have been "futurist." These interpretations pertain to John predicting future events—usually in the distant future, many centuries after his time, or even at the end of the world. Such interpretations had already become common in the early church, with people being fascinated by the vision of the "millennium"—the thousand years of peace. We say more about this in our discussion of Revelation 20. The question most often asked was, when will the millennium begin? Then, as the church became more powerful, some Christians began to say that the millennium had already begun; the question then was, when will it end?

One way or another, believers have often read Revelation as a blueprint for the course of human history, for the end of the world, or for both. Thus, at various times Christians have discovered in Revelation predictions that the end would come in the years 380, 500, 800, 1000, 1224, and many others. Some, bemoaning the corruption of the papacy, claimed that the pope was the Antichrist. Others, supporting the papacy in its struggles with the empire, claimed that that title belonged to the emperor. At the time of the Protestant Reformation, many Protestants declared the pope to be the Antichrist, and Roman Catholics countered that the Antichrist was Luther. All could see in their times the signs that John had foretold.

In more recent times, such predictions have become common again, particularly among Protestants. Once more, a number of dates have been given for the end of the world; but all have passed, and the world is still here. There were those who were certain that Hitler was the beast and that the battle against him would be the great and final Armageddon. Then others decided that this particular role belonged to the Soviet Union—a view at times espoused by high government officials in the United States. More recently some have held that the ultimate culprit is the European Common Market, or the Supreme Court, or the P.L.O., or China. . . .

There are a number of difficulties with such interpretations. The most obvious is that so many of them have been proven wrong. That should be enough to give us cause to doubt any such interpretation. But there is an even greater problem with that kind of futurist interpretation: It implies that the book had nothing to say to the many generations between John of Patmos and the interpreter. Suppose for instance that the European Common Market is the beast. That would mean that when Augustine in the fourth century, or Luther in the sixteenth, or Wesley in the eighteenth, read this book, it had nothing to say to them. It spoke of a beast that would not appear until the twentieth century! Even worse, that would mean that John, exiled in Patmos and concerned about the congregations he had left behind in Asia, wrote to them a book that they could not understand, offering no other comfort than that sometime in the future another generation would be able to understand. When you think about it, such futurist interpretations are incredibly self-centered—as if we were the only generation to whom this book is the Word of God!

Conversely, there are interpretations that place the entire significance of the book in the past. According to these interpretations, John was writing about events that were taking place in his time, or that he could foresee happening in the immediate future. He wrote to the churches in Asia to give them comfort and strength. He was not writing to anyone except those seven churches in the late first century. Thus, the only way to understand the book is to see how it relates to the situation existing at the time it was written. Any attempt to see a significance of the book for us is misguided and corrupts the purely historical research that must guide the interpretation of any ancient document.

There is much to be said for this approach. An examination of its historical setting is essential to understand Revelation. Without such examination, the book becomes a series of cryptic declarations, with visions as elusive as dreams.

Yet this approach does not suffice. We are interested in reading and interpreting this book not just because it is an interesting document of the past but also because, as Christians, we live out of the same future that John announced to his readers in Asia: the future when God's will shall be fulfilled. John reminded his readers, and reminds us still, that they had, and we have, a hope that cannot be taken away from us, a vision of what God intends for the world, and it is out of that hope and that vision that we must live our lives today. His hope, as well as ours, was grounded on certain events in the past that guaranteed the final outcome of history— events such as the incarnation, crucifixion, and resurrection of Jesus Christ.

John's hope for the future is not based on some hidden discovery of exactly how or when the end will come, but on what was then, and is today, at the very heart of the Christian faith: that we need not fear the final outcome of history, for we have seen its face in Jesus Christ. Our interest in reading his book is not futuristic, in the sense of trying to discover what will happen next. Nor is our interest merely antiquarian, in the sense of trying to discover under what conditions the book was written. We read and study Revelation because we fully expect that the God who spoke through it to Christians at the end of the first century will also speak through it to Christians at the end of the twentieth.

This requires a different method of interpretation, a method that is both historical and futuristic. We must use the historical analysis of the text and its context in order to understand what John was saying to the churches in Asia late in the first century. But that does not suffice. We must also read the book as those who share in John's faith—in his understanding of God's purposes for creation and for ourselves. John saw that these purposes had already begun to be realized and manifested in past events, notably in the work of Christ.

What John was telling his original readers is that Christians must live their lives, not out of the present pressures and expediencies, but rather out of the vision of the future that they derive from their faith. The truth is that we live most of our lives, not only out of the past, but also out of the future—what we plan to be when we grow up, where we would like to work, what we hope for our children, where we plan to retire, and so forth. Thus, a different vision of the future—a vision such as John offers in his book—should lead to a different sort of life.

Thus, in order to seek historical understanding as a means of discovering God's will, we shall begin our study of the book of Revelation.

1. The Setting
Revelation 1:1–20

TITLE AND BLESSING
Revelation 1:1–3

1:1 **The revelation of Jesus Christ, which God gave him to show his servants what must soon take place; he made it known by sending his angel to his servant John, 2 who testified to the word of God and to the testimony of Jesus Christ, even to all that he saw.**

3 Blessed is the one who reads aloud the words of the prophecy, and blessed are those who hear and who keep what is written in it; for the time is near.

As strange as it may seem to modern readers, the entirety of verses 1 and 2 are, in reality, the title of the book. As with most ancient titles, this one is a summary of the argument of the whole book, as well as of its purpose. The title also includes the name of the author.

The subject of the book is "the revelation of Jesus Christ." The word "revelation"—*apokalypsis*, which is the second word in the book and which has given it its current title—does not appear again. Yet it encapsulates all its contents, which are indeed a "revelation."

The content of this revelation, given by God to Jesus Christ, had to do with "what must soon take place." If we take this to mean that persecution will increase and Christians need to be prepared for it, then he certainly was proven right by later events. On the other hand, John apparently expected the total fulfillment of God's plan to take place in the near future, and in that case he was mistaken. Does that error invalidate his entire message? It does if, as many seem to believe, his message was a blueprint for the future, for John was wrong on the crucial matter of timing. On the other hand, if John's message is essentially a call to trust in God, in whose hands the future lies, and to resist temptation and faithless compromise on the basis of that trust, then his message is still valid, even though the end did not come when he expected. The central point in John's message is not the timing of events, but God's final triumph over evil.

Verse 2, still part of the title, does not refer to what John did in the past, apart from this book. Presumably he was already a prophet before his exile to Patmos. But normally a title such as this would be written after the book had been completed; therefore past tenses such as "testified" and "saw" refer to the actual content of the book. The means whereby this revelation was given can be depicted in the analogy of a chain whose main links are God-Jesus-the angel-John-his readers.

Then comes the first of seven blessings that appear in Revelation. (Besides the one in 1:3, the other six appear in 14:13; 16:15; 19:9; 20:6; 22:7; and 22:14.) The first blessing is twofold: It includes "the one who reads aloud," and then "those who hear and who keep what is written."

The NRSV correctly says "reads *aloud*," for what is envisioned here is that the book will be read out loud to the congregations gathered for worship. We would do well to remember this, for something is lost when words intended to be read out loud to an entire congregation in worship become the object of private study by an individual. While the private study of scripture is important and commendable, it must not take the place of public reading, for most of scripture—and certainly the book of Revelation—was originally written to be read by the community of faith as it gathered for worship. The book is addressed to them as a community, and whenever it refers to its readers as "you" we must remember that John uses the Greek plural form.

THE SALUTATION
Revelation 1:4–8

1:4 John to the seven churches that are in Asia:
Grace to you and peace from him who is and who was and who is to come, and from the seven spirits who are before his throne, 5 and from Jesus Christ, the faithful witness, the firstborn of the dead, and the ruler of the kings of the earth.
To him who loves us and freed us from our sins by his blood, 6 and made us to be a kingdom, priests serving his God and Father, to him be glory and dominion forever and ever. Amen.
7 Look! He is coming with the clouds;
every eye will see him,
even those who pierced him;
and on his account all the tribes of the earth will wail.

So it is to be. Amen.

[8] "I am the Alpha and the Omega," says the Lord God, who is and who was and who is to come, the Almighty.

This is a typical opening for a letter in the first century. Today, we begin with the date, then the name and address of the intended reader, then a greeting, the body of the letter, and finally our name. At that time, the order of a letter was somewhat different. Usually the first thing to appear was the name of the writer. Since your Bible is probably open at the beginning of Revelation, look back at the beginning of the books just before Revelation, and you will see that the Epistle of Jude begins with the word "Jude," and that the second and third epistles of John begin with "The elder." (Look back and see how many of the other epistles in the New Testament begin with the name of the writer or writers. Note also the beginning of the letter which those who were gathered in Jerusalem send in Acts 15:23.)

Next in the normal order of a letter came the name of the addressee. (Again, you may see this in the examples mentioned above.) In this case, they are "the seven churches that are in Asia." Since the number seven is used constantly in this book to denote the fullness or perfection of something, one could surmise that "the seven churches" is simply another way of referring to the entire church. We know that there were other churches in Asia at that time, at least in the cities of Colossae, Hierapolis, and Troas. Yet, we must remember that in chapters 2 and 3 John will address specific messages to each of seven churches. Thus, it would seem that the seven churches are both specific churches and a symbol that stands for the entire church.

In the typical epistolary genre, especially as it appears in the New Testament, the name of the addressee is followed by a salutation and then by a doxology. In this case, the salutation has a strange trinitarian structure, for John wishes them grace and peace "[1] from him who is and who was and who is to come, and [2] from the seven spirits who are before his throne, and [3] from Jesus Christ, the faithful witness, the firstborn of the dead, and the ruler of the kings of the earth." The reference to God as the one "who is and was and is to come" is probably a term commonly used for God in Jewish circles, for it appears in other Jewish literature of the time. The meaning of the "seven spirits" is still debated among interpreters. Most likely it is an ancient way of referring to the fullness of the Spirit. Finally, the third source of grace and peace is Jesus Christ himself. (You may wish to compare this with the typical Pauline greeting, which wishes upon his reader grace and peace from God and from Jesus Christ.)

Still before getting into the body of the letter comes a doxology—a word of praise. (Again, you may wish to compare this with Paul's letters, where after the salutation there is usually a word of praise or thanksgiving.) John's doxology here includes three main parts: first, a trinitarian word of praise (vv. 4b–6); second, a hymn of praise (v. 7); and finally a word from God (v. 8).

In such a doxology, the writer sometimes gave an indication of the main thrust of the letter. Here, it is important to note that John tells his readers at the very beginning that they have been made into "a kingdom, priests serving his God and Father." This is a reference to the promise in Exodus 19:6, "you shall be for me a priestly kingdom and a holy nation." Even more than that, it states that Christians belong to a kingdom that is not the Roman Empire and that they serve a "God and Father" who is neither the emperor in Rome nor the various interests of the surrounding society. In this regard, note that the doxology also ascribes "dominion" elsewhere than to Rome or to its representatives.

After this trinitarian formula, the doxology moves on to a hymn that is introduced with the word "Look!" John is about to tell of his visions; but he is inviting his readers to look also, so that they, like him, may see the coming triumph of Jesus and the judgment on "all the tribes of the earth." Finally, this introductory doxology ends with words from God, the one "who is and who was and who is to come," as in 1:4, and "the Almighty," which by this time was the traditional way in which Jews translated into Greek the Hebrew title of "Lord of hosts."

What God says is "I am the Alpha and the Omega." Since these are the first and last letters of the Greek alphabet, this would be like saying today, "I am from A to Z." The same expression occurs also in 21:6 and 22:13. In this case, this final word of God completes the doxology before the body of the letter.

In brief, the book of Revelation begins as a letter, and is indeed a letter addressed at the "seven churches" in Asia. (You may wish to note that the book also ends as a letter, 22:21.) Thus, although it contains a series of visions and hymns, and seven shorter letters, one to each of the seven churches in Asia, Revelation is presented in the form of a single epistle— no less so than one of the epistles of Paul.

In this letter, John makes clear that his vision is not for himself alone but is also for his original readers in the seven churches—and, by extension, for us too. He is about to tell us what "he saw" (v. 2); but he is also inviting us to "Look!" (v. 7).

THE GREAT VISION
Revelation 1:9–20

As was the case with several of the prophets of old, John's book begins with a grand vision that sets the tone for the entire book. And, also as those ancient prophets (compare for instance Isa. 6:1 and Ezek. 1:1–3), John begins by telling about the circumstances of his vision.

The Setting (1:9–11)

> 1:9 **I, John, your brother who share with you in Jesus the persecution and the kingdom and the patient endurance, was on the island called Patmos because of the word of God and the testimony of Jesus.** [10] **I was in the spirit on the Lord's day, and I heard behind me a loud voice like a trumpet** [11] **saying, "Write in a book what you see and send it to the seven churches, to Ephesus, to Smyrna, to Pergamum, to Thyatira, to Sardis, to Philadelphia, and to Laodicea."**

John identifies himself, not on the basis of a title of authority, but rather on the basis of solidarity with his readers. He is their brother and shares with them "the persecution and the kingdom and the patient endurance." The word that the NRSV translates as "persecution" can also be translated as "suffering" (NIV) or as "tribulation" (KJV). Thus, it does not necessarily imply that there was a general policy of persecuting Christians or even that there was such a policy in Asia. It certainly does mean, however, that Christians were going through difficult times.

It is significant that, together with "persecution," John mentions "the kingdom" and "patient endurance." For the general population, "the kingdom" belonged to Domitian, whose reign involved a political order in which John's readers counted for little. But John tells his readers that they share not only in tribulation but also in "the kingdom." (Remember that in 1:6 John said that Christ has "made us a kingdom.") This kingdom, though present, is hidden under the circumstances of persecution or suffering. Therefore, Christians who live with the tension between "suffering" and "the kingdom" must respond with "patient endurance," until God's purposes are fulfilled—an important reminder not only for John's readers at the time but for all of us who still live with the glorious vision of the kingdom and the sufferings and injustice of the present age.

John was on the tiny and scarcely populated island of Patmos "because of the word of God and the testimony of Jesus." He does not say literally that he had been exiled there. It is possible to understand his words to mean that he had gone there to preach. One would wonder, however, why John, who had been living in one of the most heavily populated provinces of the empire, would have felt the urge to preach in Patmos rather than in one of the many centers of population in the area. Also, there is no record or hint that there was a Christian church in Patmos in early times. Therefore, the traditional interpretation, that John was on Patmos as an exile, seems the most likely.

That he was "in the Spirit" means that he was in ecstatic communion with God and thus was ready for the vision that was about to come to him. That this was "on the Lord's day" means the first day of the week, the day of the resurrection of the Lord, the day when the church gathered to break the bread of communion. Thus it is not surprising that so much of John's vision is couched in terms of worship. Precluded from attending the present worship of his beloved churches, he sees beyond the present "persecution" to "the kingdom" and its heavenly worship. That he hears a loud voice "like a trumpet" is fitting in this setting, for throughout the Old Testament the trumpet signifies the cultic presence of God (see, for instance, Leviticus 23:24: "a holy convocation commemorated with trumpet blasts").

What the voice says sets John's agenda for his entire book: He is to write what he sees and send it to "the seven churches," which are then listed. (On these seven churches, collectively and individually, see our comments on 2:1–3:22.)

The Vision (1:12–20)

1:12 **Then I turned to see whose voice it was that spoke to me, and on turning I saw seven golden lampstands,** 13 **and in the midst of the lampstands I saw one like the Son of Man, clothed with a long robe and with a golden sash across his chest.** 14 **His head and his hair were white as white wool, white as snow; his eyes were like a flame of fire,** 15 **his feet were like burnished bronze, refined as in a furnace, and his voice was like the sound of many waters.** 16 **In his right hand he held seven stars, and from his mouth came a sharp, two-edged sword, and his face was like the sun shining with full force.**

17 **When I saw him, I fell at his feet as though dead. But he placed his right hand on me, saying, "Do not be afraid; I am the first and the last,** 18 **and the living one. I was dead, and see, I am alive forever and ever; and I have the keys of Death and of Hades.** 19 **Now write what you have seen, what is, and what is to take place after this.** 20 **As for the mystery of the seven stars that you saw in my right hand, and the seven golden lampstands: the seven stars are the angels of the seven churches, and the seven lampstands are the seven churches.**

This entire passage is reminiscent of Daniel 7:13–14 and 10:5–10 (which you may wish to read as background). The seven lampstands, as John is told at the end of the vision, symbolize the seven churches to which he is to write. The fact that the "one like the Son of Man" is "in the midst of the lampstands" means that "the heavenly Christ is no absentee landlord. He is present in his earthly communities" (Harrington, *Revelation*, 52).

The description of the One whom John sees is majestic and patterned after Daniel 10. He is dressed in the typical attire of a high priest or of someone in very high office. His white hair and blazing eyes are signs both of his great age and of perennial strength and authority. His feet are made of a metal alloy that the NRSV translates as "burnished bronze" but which probably refers to a gold alloy that was almost as valuable as gold and may have been a product for which Thyatira was known. His voice, compared in Daniel with "the roar of a multitude," here is "like the sound of many waters."

The seven stars that he holds in his right hand, we are told later (1:20), are "the angels of the seven churches." There is much debate as to what or who these angels may be. (See the commentary on 2:1.) In any case, what the reference means here is that he holds even now the seven churches in his hand and thus cares for them and has power over them. The two-edged sword coming from his mouth is a common image for the Word of God, which is the only—and more than sufficient—weapon this figure carries. Finally, the face "like the sun shining with full force" is a reference to the divine glory, on which no one can gaze and live (Ex. 33:20).

No wonder, then, that John falls "as though dead" before this majestic vision. And great wonder, then, that the majestic figure—who is none other than Christ in his full glory—stoops to touch him and says, "Do not be afraid"!

There are two important points to be made about this vision, for they clarify John's message and theology. First, this is a vision of Christ, as Christ himself will immediately explain: "I was dead, and see, I am alive forever and ever." Yet this Christ is also presented as the Almighty, the Ancient of Days, the One who has the keys of Death and of the place of the dead (Hades, in 1:18). Throughout his book, John emphasizes the majestic power of Jesus, the Christ, the Lamb who was slain, and John speaks of that power in terms that are clearly divine.

Second, notice the startling good news the passage conveys. We tend either to think of the Mighty One in terms so majestic that there is a chasm between the divine Being and us, or to cut God down to size so that we may feel more comfortable in the divine presence. But here John presents us with an overpowering vision of Christ's majesty and might—so brilliant that "his face was like the sun shining with full force"—and yet this mighty Christ stoops to touch John and says, "Do not be afraid." This means not only "do not be afraid of me" but also that, since Christ holds "the keys of Death and of Hades" and since Christ is with you, there is nothing, absolutely nothing, of which you should be afraid. To John, exiled in Patmos, and to his first readers suffering in a hostile society, this must have been good news indeed. And so it should be for us, for this is the Gospel!

2. Letters to Seven Churches
Revelation 2:1–3:22

We come now to what is perhaps the best-known part of the book of Revelation: the seven letters addressed to the seven churches, which were listed in 1:11. Some introductory remarks may help us to understand these letters.

First, it is important to note that, as far as we know, these letters never circulated separately. They were always part of the larger epistle that is the entire book of Revelation. In this, they are similar to comments that we find occasionally in the letters of Paul, or even in our own letters, when we write to an entire family and at some point, say, "John and Mary, please remember that . . ." This means that, although each of the so-called letters is addressed to a specific congregation, all of the recipients of John's book would hear what was being said to each of the seven churches.

Second, note the common structure of all seven letters:

1. In each one, John is commanded to write "to the angel of the church in [Ephesus, Smyrna, Thyatira, etc.]." There has been much debate as to what may be meant by the "angel" of a church. Some suggest that this means simply the leader of the church. But such use of the term "angel" would be rather surprising. Throughout the book of Revelation, the term "angel" is used to refer to "a heavenly being who serves God." For that reason, most scholars interpret these "angels" of specific churches as a reflection of the commonly held view at the time: that nations, cities, families and, in this case, churches, had their heavenly counterparts, or "angels." The message is sent to these angels, to be delivered to the churches.
2. Each letter begins by declaring that what follows is "the words of," and this is then followed by a metaphoric description of Jesus. In several cases, the description itself is taken from the great vision in chapter 1. Also, in most of the letters it is possible to see the con-

nection between the way Christ is described and what follows in the body of the letter. In any case, it is significant to note that the Greek words translated as "the words of" had an archaic sound even in John's time and were the standard way in which Greek-speaking Jews translated the phrase of the Old Testament prophets, "thus saith the Lord."

3. The body of the letter begins with the words "I know," followed in most cases by "your works," but in two others by "where you are living" or by "your afflictions and your poverty." The body then includes words of commendation and/or condemnation, often stated in terms that relate to the specific conditions under which that particular church exists.

4. Finally, each letter concludes with a promise to those who "conquer," either preceded or followed by the phrase—which appears in all seven letters—"Let anyone who has an ear listen to what the Spirit is saying to the churches." The use of the plural, "churches," indicates that each of these letters was to be read to all the churches and that each church was expected to overhear what the Spirit said to the others. Thus, although there are seven distinct, specific messages, in a sense they are all addressed to the entire church.

EPHESUS
Revelation 2:1–7

2:1 "To the angel of the church in Ephesus write: These are the words of him who holds the seven stars in his right hand, who walks among the seven golden lampstands:

2 "I know your works, your toil and your patient endurance. I know that you cannot tolerate evildoers; you have tested those who claim to be apostles but are not, and have found them to be false. 3 I also know that you are enduring patiently and bearing up for the sake of my name, and that you have not grown weary. 4 But I have this against you, that you have abandoned the love you had at first. 5 Remember then from what you have fallen; repent, and do the works you did at first. If not, I will come to you and remove your lampstand from its place, unless you repent. 6 Yet this is to your credit: you hate the works of the Nicolaitans, which I also hate. 7 Let anyone who has an ear listen to what the Spirit is saying to the churches. To everyone who conquers, I will give permission to eat from the tree of life that is in the paradise of God.

The first church to be addressed is the one in Ephesus. There are probably several reasons for this. First, according to several ancient Christian writers, John lived in Ephesus prior to his exile in Patmos. Therefore, he begins his seven letters by writing to his own home church. Second, when returning to the mainland from Patmos, one would normally head for the seaport of Ephesus. Thus, the messenger carrying John's book—as we have seen, the entire book is an epistle—would visit Ephesus first. The order of the other churches addressed follows a vast circle, as if the messenger were expected to take the main road leading north along the coast to Smyrna and on to Pergamum, there to take the southeastern road that led, in order, to Thyatira, Sardis, Philadelphia, and Laodicea (and eventually to return to Ephesus following the valley of the westward-flowing river Meander). Finally, the church at Ephesus is addressed first because it was the "mother church" of the others and because Ephesus itself was by far the largest city in the region.

Ephesus was a large seaport and a center of trade with the interior of Asia. In the entire eastern portion of the Roman Empire, only Alexandria and Antioch rivaled that city. Ephesus was famous for its huge temple to Artemis (or Diana), one of the seven wonders of the ancient world. It was also famous for its books of magic—to the point that all such books, whether coming from Ephesus or not, were called "Ephesine books." The city boasted a large Jewish population whose power and prestige were such that it was awarded local citizenship.

All of these elements had played an important role in the development of the Christian church in Ephesus, as the book of Acts tells the story (Acts 19). There we are told that upon arriving at Ephesus, Paul found "some disciples" who apparently were more followers of John the Baptist than of Christ, and we are also told how Paul preached in the synagogue until he was expelled. Then there is an episode leading to the burning of the books of magic that were worth an enormous sum. Finally, the preaching of Paul and his companions is seen as threatening the lucrative business of the silversmiths, who profited from making small reproductions of the temple of Artemis, and the outcome is a riot in the theater, which only the intervention of the town clerk can stop.

John is told to write to the Ephesian church on behalf of "him who holds the seven stars in his right hand, who walks among the seven golden lampstands"—a reference to the vision that John has just described. To a church in a rich and powerful city, the mother church of the others in the area, it was important to know that its Lord still walked among the "lampstands"—that is, the churches—and held that church, as well as the "angels" of the other churches, in his right hand.

The message to Ephesus is generally positive. The church there is praised for its steadfastness, particularly with reference to the challenge posed by "those who claim to be apostles but are not" (2:2) and by "the Nicolaitans" (2:6). The false apostles were probably itinerant preachers who went from place to place, demanding that the church support them. As we know from other writings of approximately the same time, the early church had difficulty distinguishing between those who were genuine apostles—that is, preachers who traveled carrying the gospel—and those who simply wished to live off the hospitality of Christian communities. In Paul's letters, the "false apostles" or "super-apostles" are those who contradicted his preaching of salvation by grace (2 Cor. 11:5, 13). Yet, it is impossible to tell exactly who are the "false apostles" in this message to Ephesus, and therefore it is possible that they may be the Nicolaitans.

The Nicolaitans are mentioned also in 2:15—the message to Pergamum—again with no explanation as to their teachings. A possible explanation as to who they were may be found in the meaning of the name Nicolaus, "conqueror of the people," which may be taken to be a translation of Balaam, "he destroyed the people." Thus, when in the message to Pergamum there is reference to "the teaching of Balaam" (2:14) and to "the Nicolaitans" (2:15), it is quite possible that these are two terms for the same thing.

The story of Balaam appears in Numbers 22—24. Briefly told, he was a prophet of God hired by the king of Moab to curse the Israelites. He eventually agreed to go to Moab, but he insisted that he would speak only what God gave him to speak, with the result that instead of cursing the Israelites he blessed them. Even so, when the Israelites defeated Moab, they killed Balaam, presumably because he was in the service of the king of Moab. From that point on, Balaam became a negative figure in Israelite history, on the basis that he had hired himself out to the enemy, even though God would not let him prophesy against Israel (see Deut. 23:4–5). He was said to practice divination (Josh. 24:9–10), and by the time we get to the beginning of the Christian era, he had become the symbol of the mercenary prophet. Thus, in 2 Peter 2:15–16 we read of "Balaam son of Bosor, who loved the wages of doing wrong, but was rebuked for his own transgression."

All of this fits very well with what we know of John of Patmos and of his concern that Christians not compromise their faith. The pressures to compromise came not only—and probably not even primarily—from the state but also from society and its economic structures. Those who did compromise, claiming that they could participate in the various rituals of the society and yet remain faithful, would then be seen as following the example of Balaam, who was willing to go into the service of the king of Moab but insisted on speaking nothing but the will of God. Balaam was partly successful, in that God would not allow him to curse the Israelites, but still he paid for his actions with his life.

In conclusion, it is quite likely that the Nicolaitans are the same as the "followers of Balaam" and also the followers of "the woman Jezebel" in Thyatira (2:20). But, no matter who the Nicolaitans may have been, the message to Ephesus clearly commends the church there for having stood firmly against them.

But not all is well in Ephesus. The message to that church says "but I have this against you, that you have abandoned the love you had at first" (2:4). Most interpreters agree that this refers to the love within the community of faith, rather than to their love of God—the very fact that they resisted the "false prophets" and the Nicolaitans would be seen as a sign of their love for God and God's truth. These Ephesians were staunch defenders of the truth, but in that defense they had lost much of the love they should have had for each other. This is a phenomenon with which we are all familiar, for it has happened repeatedly in the history of the church and continues to happen to this day. Christians who are rightly concerned about the purity of faith and doctrine can become so obsessed by that concern that they begin looking at each other askance, and love is set aside. Orthodoxy becomes the hallmark of the "true faith," and love seems to be of secondary importance.

We might think that this is no great sin. After all, we could say, we are all human. But the message to Ephesus tells us otherwise. The Lord tells them: "I will come to you and remove your lampstand from its place, unless you repent." This is serious business. The church in Ephesus—the mother of all the churches in Asia, zealous for orthodoxy, and resistant to all the temptations to compromise with the evils of society—could be destroyed, not because it has lost the pure doctrine or because it has compromised with the world but because love no longer reigns in it. This is a word that today's church must also heed, for we too may be tempted to set so much store on our correct theology and proper process of church government that we risk forgetting that a church without love is already dead.

To those who conquer, that is, those who avoid both the mercenary compromise of the Nicolaitans and the temptation to loveless orthodoxy, the Spirit promises that they will eat of "the tree of life." Some interpreters suggest that this particular promise alludes to Ephesian coins, which carried an engraving of the sacred tree of Artemis. Thus, those who refuse to make a compromise for the sake of those Ephesian coins (and the tree depicted on them) will be rewarded with the much more valuable tree of life. In Genesis 3:22–24, God decides to expel Adam and Eve from Eden, so that they might not "take also from the tree of life, and eat, and live forever." Thus, what was forbidden in Genesis is now promised in Revelation! Presumably, now those who conquer through love will be ready to live forever in communion with God and with one another. This is dealt with more fully in reference to 22:2.

SMYRNA
Revelation 2:8–11

> 2:8 "And to the angel of the church in Smyrna write: These are the words of the first and the last, who was dead and came to life:
> ⁹ "I know your affliction and your poverty, even though you are rich. I know the slander on the part of those who say that they are Jews and are not, but are a synagogue of Satan. ¹⁰ Do not fear what you are about to suffer. Beware, the devil is about to throw some of you into prison so that you may be tested, and for ten days you will have affliction. Be faithful until death, and I will give you the crown of life. ¹¹ Let anyone who has an ear listen to what the Spirit is saying to the churches. Whoever conquers will not be harmed by the second death.

Of the seven cities in Asia to which these seven messages are addressed, Smyrna is the only one that today is a flourishing, major city—the Turkish Izmir. That has to do with its location as a major seaport protected by a deep gulf. (In the case of Ephesus, the ancient seaport has been filled with silt to such an extent that the ruins of Ephesus now lie several miles from the sea.) Indeed, Smyrna's prime location caused it to be rebuilt after it had been destroyed by the neighboring Lydians and had stood as an abandoned site for several centuries. For that reason, it was sometimes called "the city that died yet lives." Significantly, this message to Smyrna is dominated by the theme of life and death. Christ is described as "the first and the last, who was dead and came to life." Christians are exhorted to be "faithful until death." And those who conquer "will not be harmed by the second death."

At the time Revelation was written, Smyrna's most majestic buildings surrounded a hill, so that as one sailed into its port, one would see what appeared to be a crown of buildings. Hence, poets spoke of "the crown of Smyrna." That is probably also why the promise for those who are "faithful until death" is that they will receive "the crown of life."

Once one understands these allusions, one can easily see the counter-cultural and even subversive nature of the message. Smyrna is proud of its crown of buildings and of its having risen after its own death. But even Smyrna and all that are in it will eventually die. They will die a death from which there is no recovery, the "second death" (on this subject see 20:14–15). Smyrna's crown of buildings is impressive but is really nothing when compared with the crown of life believers are promised. The message to Smyrna turns things upside down, so to speak, so that those things on which the city prides itself are nothing when compared with what is promised to faithful Christians.

If we were to write a similar message to our churches today, what would we say? What are the elements in our society and culture on which we pride ourselves? Should they appear differently when viewed from a Christian perspective? Do they?

Then there is a second element of reversal in the letter. The city of Smyrna was rich. In it, there was a relatively poor community of believers who suffered not only poverty but some form of "affliction" that the message does not specify. This was probably political and social pressure—to the point that the message says some of the believers will be thrown into prison. But the message says that they are in fact rich and that after "ten days"—meaning a relatively short time, as compared to eternity—they will be conquerors and receive the crown of life.

Again, this reversal of perspective is quite relevant for the church today. In various parts of the world, and in some sectors of Western society, there are very poor churches. Sometimes we tend to think that, because they do not have as many financial resources as we do, they have little to contribute to the church at large. Significantly, this message to the church in Smyrna, a church that was apparently poor, is the most positive of all seven messages. That should give us pause as we make judgments about churches in various situations today.

Finally, there is a third reversal in the message—a reversal about which we must be careful. It has to do with those "who say they are Jews and are not, but are a synagogue of Satan" (2:9). It is impossible to know precisely who these supposedly false Jews were. Most probably they were simply Jews who had refused to accept the Christian message and who insisted that the Christian community in Smyrna—probably still mostly Jewish—were not true Jews. We know that there was a sizable Jewish population in Smyrna.

Several decades after the writing of Revelation, Polycarp, the bishop of Smyrna, who according to tradition had been a disciple of John, was martyred. In the record of his martyrdom there are indications of bitter conflicts between Jews and Christians. According to that document, after Polycarp's death, the Jews of the city tried to prevent the Christians from claiming his body, arguing that they probably would hide it and claim that he had risen, as they had done with Jesus. As is apparent from Revelation 2:9, that bitter enmity between Christians and Jews in Smyrna existed for some time.

Such enmity would have serious practical consequences. The Roman authorities were well aware of Judaism and its believers' refusal to worship foreign gods. The authorities had reluctantly come to accept what to them seemed a strange idiosyncratic notion, so that Jews were not expected to participate in the various religious ceremonies normally connected with social, political, and economic life. As long as Christianity was considered a sect within Judaism, Christians could enjoy that measure of protection. But as soon as they were perceived to follow a different religion, there was increasing danger of persecution. Thus there were two reasons for Christians to claim that they were in fact Jews: (1) the theological reason, which allowed Christians to claim for themselves the Hebrew scriptures, including the promises made to Abraham and his heirs, and (2) the political reason, which afforded Christians the same exemption from various religious observances as the Jews had. Those were reasons for the obviously bitter battle for the title of Jews that stands behind the comments in 2:9 about false Jews and a "synagogue of Satan."

Eventually things changed drastically, to the point that Christians had the upper hand. And, if John could fault Jews for refusing to protect Christians at an earlier time, Christians can be faulted with far more reason for refusing to protect Jews in more recent centuries. Thus, we must take care lest we use the words in Revelation—as they have been used—as an excuse to continue practicing or promoting discrimination against Jews.

PERGAMUM
Revelation 2:12–17

2:12 **"And to the angel of the church in Pergamum write: These are the words of him who has the sharp two-edged sword:**

13 **"I know where you are living, where Satan's throne is. Yet you are holding fast to my name, and you did not deny your faith in me even in the**

days of Antipas my witness, my faithful one, who was killed among you, where Satan lives. [14] But I have a few things against you: you have some there who hold to the teaching of Balaam, who taught Balak to put a stumbling block before the people of Israel, so that they would eat food sacrificed to idols and practice fornication. [15] So you also have some who hold to the teaching of the Nicolaitans. [16] Repent then. If not, I will come to you soon and make war against them with the sword of my mouth. [17] Let anyone who has an ear listen to what the Spirit is saying to the churches. To everyone who conquers I will give some of the hidden manna, and I will give a white stone, and on the white stone is written a new name that no one knows except the one who receives it.

Pergamum appears to have been the seat of Roman administration in the province of Asia—although the governor usually resided in Ephesus, a much larger and more comfortable city. That may be why here it is called "where Satan's throne is." But more probably that epithet refers to the intensity of pagan worship there. Pergamum was noted for a great temple of Zeus, whose ruins can still be seen. Just outside the city stood a vast complex of buildings devoted to the god of healing, Asclepius; this complex served as an ancient hospital, in which religion and healing were brought together. Pergamum also was the first city in Asia to build a temple in honor of the emperor (29 B.C.). Therefore, one should not wonder that Christians there had a difficult time—to the point that at some time before John's writing, a Christian by the name of Antipas, about whom no more is known, had paid for his faith with his life.

Under such circumstances, those who preached accommodation to the existing order apparently gained a hearing in the church. These are those whom our text calls "Nicolaitans" who "hold to the teaching of Balaam." We have already met them while studying the message to the Ephesians (2:1–7). (See the explanation of these names in the discussion on that passage.) But while the church in Ephesus rejected such teaching, the one in Pergamum made room for them.

In that setting, the feature from the great original vision that is picked up in order to describe Christ is that he "has the sharp two-edged sword" (see 1:16). This is the Word of God, the only weapon Christ wields, but a weapon sharp enough to destroy those who will not repent (2:16).

The reward for those who conquer is described as "hidden manna" and as a white stone with a new name written on it. The hidden manna refers to a late Jewish tradition according to which the manna, bread from heaven, will be food in the final heavenly banquet. Since Christians understood communion as a foretaste of that banquet, this would remind believers in Pergamum that when they participated in communion, even in the midst of grave difficulties, they were receiving a glimpse, or having a foretaste, of the banquet of the Lamb. The white stone is a sign of victory—in ancient times, "white" meant "victory," just as for us it means "purity." Note that the "new name" is given by Christ in reward for "holding fast to my name" (2:13). This means that those who conquer by holding fast to the name of Christ will be rewarded with a new reality, a new life.

Few of us know the hardships of trying to live as Christians in a hostile environment. Yet, even in our day and in our more favorable environment, we must ask ourselves if we are not tempted to make compromises similar to those of the Nicolaitans. If it was unacceptable for Christians in Pergamum, where they risked death, to make such compromises, could we really think that our own compromises are legitimate?

THYATIRA
Revelation 2:18–29

2:18 "And to the angel of the church in Thyatira write: These are the words of the Son of God, who has eyes like a flame of fire, and whose feet are like burnished bronze:
¹⁹ "I know your works—your love, faith, service, and patient endurance. I know that your last works are greater than the first. ²⁰ But I have this against you: you tolerate that woman Jezebel, who calls herself a prophet and is teaching and beguiling my servants to practice fornication and to eat food sacrificed to idols. ²¹ I gave her time to repent, but she refuses to repent of her fornication. ²² Beware, I am throwing her on a bed, and those who commit adultery with her I am throwing into great distress, unless they repent of her doings; ²³ and I will strike her children dead. And all the churches will know that I am the one who searches minds and hearts, and I will give to each of you as your works deserve. ²⁴ But to the rest of you in Thyatira, who do not hold this teaching, who have not learned what some call 'the deep things of Satan,' to you I say, I do not lay on you any other burden; ²⁵ only hold fast to what you have until I come. ²⁶ To everyone who conquers and continues to do my works to the end,
        I will give authority over the nations;
    ²⁷ to rule them with an iron rod,
        as when clay pots are shattered—
²⁸ even as I also received authority for my Father. To the one who conquers I will also give the morning star. ²⁹ Let anyone who has an ear listen to what the Spirit is saying to the churches.

Thyatira was an unprotected, militarily weak, but commercially prosperous city. It was known for its industry, particularly the smelting of bronze and the production of articles of leather, pottery, weaving, and dyeing. (Remember that Lydia, the seller of purple dye in Acts, was from Thyatira.) As was usual throughout the area, people who practiced such crafts were organized into guilds, which strengthened their inner bonds by offering worship and sacrifices to their patron god and which showed their loyalty to the emperor by participating in his worship. Although these guilds were legal, the Roman Empire had a deep-seated fear of private clubs, which were always suspected as being seats of conspiracy and subversion.

Christians were especially hard-pressed in Thyatira, a fairly small town where one had to belong to a guild in order to make a living. It is not surprising that the urge for Christians to compromise their faith was strong.

In the message to Thyatira, Christ describes himself as the one "who has eyes like a flame of fire, and whose feet are like burnished bronze." Both of these images bring to mind the smelting industry of the city. They also indicate that Christ is firm on his feet and that no one can escape the gaze of his eyes. Thus, this description at the beginning of the message is a warning to the Thyatirans.

The letter to Thyatira, like that to Pergamum, stands in sharp contrast to the letter to Ephesus. The Ephesians rejected the teaching of the Nicolaitans but lost their original love for one another. The Thyatirans are praised because their love, faith, service, and patient endurance—in short, their "works"—"are greater than the first." In other words, they have moved in exactly the opposite direction than have the Ephesians. But— and in this also they stand in contrast to the Ephesians—they have succumbed to the enticements of compromise with the world around them, to the point of falling into idolatry.

This is what is meant by "you tolerate that woman Jezebel," which probably refers to the same sort of teaching that the messages to the churches ascribe elsewhere to Balaam and to the Nicolaitans. In this case, they seem to have been prompted by a woman who claimed the title of prophet but whom John calls "Jezebel"—not her real name—in order to connect her teachings with the notorious queen of Israel who led the nation astray (see her story in 1 Kings 18—21 and 2 Kings 9). As in the case of Jezebel, "fornication" here probably does not mean sexual immortality but rather the worship of idols—which in the entire prophetic tradition was considered adultery against God.

The conflict with this so-called Jezebel apparently had been going on for some time, for the message says "I gave her time to repent." In any case, she and her followers will be punished by being thrown onto a bed of suffering—meaning a sickbed, in ironic contrast to the bed of their adulteries—and will suffer death. This will be an appropriate punishment, because "the one who searches minds and hearts"—with "eyes like a flame of fire"—"will give to each of you as your works deserve."

This does not mean, however, that all in Thyatira are lost. On the contrary, this letter, like all the others, concludes with a promise for those who conquer. In this case, the promise is that they will share in the authority of the Messiah.

In brief, while the message to Ephesus warns the church about the dangers of loveless orthodoxy, the message to Thyatira warns against the dangers of a "soft" love that tolerates all things and judges none. Again, this is a timely message for the churches not only in the first century but also in ours.

SARDIS
Revelation 3:1–6

3:1 "And to the angel of the church in Sardis write: These are the words of him who has the seven spirits of God and the seven stars:

"I know your works; you have a name of being alive, but you are dead. [2] Wake up, and strengthen what remains and is on the point of death, for I have not found your works perfect in the sight of my God. [3] Remember then what you received and heard; obey it, and repent. If you do not wake up, I will come like a thief, and you will not know at what hour I will come to you. [4] Yet you have still a few persons in Sardis who have not soiled their clothes; they will walk with me, dressed in white, for they are worthy. [5] If you conquer, you will be clothed like them in white robes, and I will not blot your name out of the book of life; I will confess your name before my Father and before his angels. [6] Let anyone who has an ear listen to what the Spirit is saying to the churches.

We continue along the southeasterly road that we took at Pergamum and have already passed through Thyatira. Beyond Sardis, where we now are, the road leads to Philadelphia and finally to Laodicea.

Sardis was a relatively prosperous city that, however, had seen better days. In the sixth century B.C., it had been the home of the fabulously rich Croesus—to whom the saying "as rich as Croesus" refers. At the time of Revelation, Sardis was still fairly affluent, because it was the meeting place of several trade routes, and the plains below it were fertile. All in all, it probably was a comfortable but unexciting place to live. The city itself, built atop a hill and well fortified, had never been taken by assault. That, however, had not always kept the enemy out, for twice—first in 549 B.C. and again in 195 B.C.—it had been taken by stealth.

The message to Sardis reveals a church very similar to the city itself. It too had seen better days and now apparently was coasting on its past achievements. There was nothing particularly wrong with it; there is no mention here of Balaam or Jezebel, of idolatry or even of opposition from anybody. But still, everything was wrong with it! The words are damning: "You have a name of being alive, but you are dead."

The complacency of the church in Sardis is subtly compared with the complacency of the city when it trusted its own defenses and found itself taken by the enemy: "If you do not wake up, I will come like a thief, and you will not know at what hour I will come to you" (compare with Matt. 24:42–44, Luke 12:39–40, 1 Thess. 5:2–4, 2 Peter 3:10, Rev. 16:15). The only solution for the church at large, as for a city whose enemy seeks to enter, is to wake up and be watchful.

Yet not all in Sardis have fallen into this sort of spiritual stupor. There are still some "who have not soiled their clothes." To them it is promised that they will walk with Christ, "dressed in white." To the rest of the church, the message is that, if they awake, repent and "conquer," they too will be robed in white, their names will remain in "the book of life," and Christ will confess their names—that is, intercede for them—before the Father and the angels. (The "book of life" appears repeatedly in Revelation. Besides here, it is mentioned in 13:8; 17:8; 20:12, 15; 21:27. Paul also refers to it in Philippians 4:3. The image refers to the practice of keeping lists of people who are authorized to enter a certain place or to enjoy certain privileges. A modern equivalent is the voter registration printout; if your name is not on it, you cannot vote.)

In all of this, there are overtones that would constantly remind the believers in Sardis of their baptism. For one, the term "name" appears repeatedly. They have the "name" of being alive. In verse 4, where the NRSV says that a few "persons" have not soiled their garments, the Greek says is a few "names." Then there is the reference to one's "name" written in the book of life and also to one's "name" being confessed before God and the angels. From ancient times, baptism was connected with naming—not necessarily, as later became customary, with calling the person "Mary" or "Peter" or "Susan," but rather with sealing them with the name of Jesus Christ, thereby receiving the name of "Christian." (A few years after

John's message to Sardis, a Roman governor from a nearby province wrote to the emperor asking if Christians should be punished merely for the "name," or for some crime in particular. On their part, many Christian martyrs declared that they were ready to suffer death for the "name.")

But even more than in this repeated use of the term "name," the baptismal overtones of this message may be seen in its repeated references to white, clean garments (see vv. 4 and 5). It was customary in the ancient church, when believers came out of the waters of baptism, to dress them in a new, white garment to indicate the beginning of a new life of purity and victory. Those who "have not soiled their clothes" have kept the vows of their baptism, and their "white robes" as they walk with Christ are the fulfillment of the victory begun at their baptism. Thus, what the message is saying to those in Sardis who have fallen asleep is that they must remember what they have received and heard (v. 3), particularly at their own baptism, and repent. (At this point one is reminded of Martin Luther, who said that when he felt sorely tempted he would cry out, "I am baptized!")

The church in Sardis sounds sadly familiar in our days. As one looks around, one sees many churches where there is a semblance of life, a sort of "coasting" on past glories and achievements, the sort of assurance that the sentinels on the walls of Sardis must have felt before the city was taken by the enemy. There is nothing wrong with such churches. And yet, everything is wrong with them! What can we do in such cases? The call to Sardis is still valid: "Remember then what you have received and heard; obey it, and repent."

PHILADELPHIA
Revelation 3:7–13

3:7 "And to the angel of the church in Philadelphia write:
These are the words of the holy one, the true one,
who has the key of David,
who opens and no one will shut,
who shuts and no one opens:
8 "I know your works. Look, I have set before you an open door, which no one is able to shut. I know that you have but little power, and yet you have kept my word and have not denied my name. 9 I will make those of the synagogue of Satan who say that they are Jews and are not, but are lying— I will make them come and bow down before your feet, and they will learn that I have loved you. 10 Because you have kept my word of patient endurance, I will keep you from the hour of trial that is coming on the whole

world to test the inhabitants of the earth. [11] I am coming soon; hold fast to what you have, so that no one may seize your crown. [12] If you conquer, I will make you a pillar in the temple of my God; you will never go out of it. I will write on you the name of my God, and the name of the city of my God, the new Jerusalem that comes down from my God out of heaven, and my own new name. [13] Let anyone who has an ear listen to what the Spirit is saying to the churches.

Philadelphia was a relatively small city, founded as a Greek colony as a means to Hellenize the area. It also had a fairly large and apparently influential Jewish community, which had decided that Christians were not true children of Abraham. This conflict with the synagogue takes up part of the message to the Philadelphians and in many ways is similar to what we saw in the message to Smyrna (see discussion on 2:8–11). Apparently it did not end there, for some fifteen years later Bishop Ignatius of Antioch, writing to the Philadelphians, warns them against "interpretations regarding Judaism." He makes it clear, however, that this is not an indictment of Jews as such, but rather of Judaizing interpretations of Christianity (*Letter to the Philadelphians*, 6:1).

The message to the Philadelphians, like that to the Smyrneans, has no words of criticism or condemnation but only of praise and promise. The description of Christ, unlike those in the other messages, is not taken directly from the initial grand vision. Rather, it is tailored to meet the challenge posed by the conflict with the synagogue. Christ is "the holy one, the true one." These are titles a good Jew would reserve only for God. Thus, the message is affirming the absolute and final authority of Christ.

In 1:18 we were told that Christ has "the keys of Death and of Hades." Now we are told the counterpart of that: He also has the key of David and thus the power to determine who can enter into the messianic kingdom. With this key he has put before the Philadelphians "an open door, which no one can shut." Although in other contexts the image of an open door refers to missionary opportunities (for instance, Acts 14:27 and 2 Cor. 2:12), here it is used as a word of comfort for those who have been excluded from the synagogue, told that they do not belong to the people of God. That is also the significance of the promise of being made "a pillar in the temple of my God; you will never go out of it." In the temple in Jerusalem, no Gentile could enter. In this temple that Christ promises, these Christians, rejected and excluded by the synagogue, will have a place so permanent that it is like a column that no one can remove.

Furthermore, says Christ, "I will write on you the name of my God, and the name of the city of my God." In the building of some temples, wealthy contributors had their names inscribed on a column to indicate that this particular column had been placed there because of their support. Such inscriptions usually included also the name of the city and the god to whom the temple was dedicated. Now these Philadelphian Christians are told not only that Christ has the key to open their admission to the temple and that they will be permanent fixtures there, as immovable as columns, but also that they will bear the inscription that will tell all that they were placed there by none other than God!

In the middle of the letter (v. 9) there are words that sound horribly harsh, to the effect that those who now harass Christians saying that they are not true Jews will have to "come and bow down before your feet." Significantly, what John has done is simply to turn around what some of the Jewish prophets said about those who in their time harassed and oppressed their people. See, for instance, Isaiah 60:14: "The descendants of those who oppressed you shall come bending low to you, and all who despised you shall bow down at your feet." Any who oppress others will see their situation reversed—that those who think they are "insiders" with God had better watch out lest they find themselves out in the cold!

LAODICEA
Revelation 3:14–22

3:14 "And to the angel of the church in Laodicea write: The words of the Amen, the faithful and true witness, the origin of God's creation:
15 "I know your works; you are neither cold nor hot. I wish that you were either cold or hot. 16 So, because you are lukewarm, and neither cold nor hot, I am about to spit you out of my mouth. 17 For you say, 'I am rich, I have prospered, and I need nothing.' You do not realize that you are wretched, pitiable, poor, blind, and naked. 18 Therefore I counsel you to buy from me gold refined by fire so that you may be rich; and white robes to clothe you and to keep the shame of your nakedness from being seen; and salve to anoint your eyes so that you may see. 19 I reprove and discipline those whom I love. Be earnest, therefore, and repent. 20 Listen! I am standing at the door, knocking; if you hear my voice and open the door, I will come in to you and eat with you, and you with me. 21 To the one who conquers I will give a place with me on my throne, just as I myself conquered and sat down with my Father on his throne. 22 Let anyone who has an ear listen to what the Spirit is saying to the churches."

Laodicea, the last city John's letter-carrying messenger would visit, was a rich city. It was sufficiently rich that when the city was destroyed by an earthquake, some thirty-five years before John's writing, its inhabitants proudly refused imperial aid and rebuilt their destroyed buildings out of the city's own resources. In the year 100, just a few years after John's vision and messages, another earthquake destroyed Laodicea; once again, the city was rebuilt without outside help.

The sources of the city's wealth and fame were many. Among them, however, three stood out: banking; a product known as "Phrygian powder," from which a medicinal eye salve was made; and a shiny black wool from which luxurious black apparel was woven.

The city's one outstanding shortcoming was its water. A few miles to the southeast was Colossae, famous for its cool mineral springs. To the north, across the deep and narrow valley of the river Lycus, a visitor standing on the ruins of Laodicea can still see the much more imposing ruins of Hierapolis and the white cliffs known today as Pamukkale, the "cotton castle." That city was famous for its hot medicinal waters, which brought hundreds of visitors seeking cures for a variety of ailments. The water spilling over the mountainside from Hierapolis produced the beautiful mineral deposits whose many tiers of white rock gave the "cotton castle" its name. That water was piped to Laodicea—where some remnants of the water system can still be seen—but by the time it arrived there, its tepidness and mineral content made the water nauseating.

All of this stands behind the devastating message to the church in Laodicea. Apparently, that church had no problems—and that precisely was its problem. The message starts with an allusion to the one sore point in the city's reputation: "You are neither cold nor hot. I wish that you were either cold or hot. So, because you are lukewarm, and neither cold nor hot, I am about to spit you out of my mouth."

Then the message takes those things of which Laodiceans were most proud and turns them around: "For you say, 'I am rich, I have prospered, and I need nothing.' You do not realize that you are wretched, pitiable, poor, blind, and naked." The rich and proud banking city is "wretched, pitiable, poor." The city famous for its eye salve and for its luxurious clothing is "blind and naked." The solution for Christians there is to cease trusting on these things, or on their own resources and wealth, or on their fine wool and their famous salve, and "to buy from me gold refined by fire so that you may be rich; and white robes to clothe you and to keep the shame of your nakedness from being seen; and salve to anoint your eyes so that you may see."

The next verse (19) includes the only positive line in the entire message: "I reprove and discipline those whom I love." In other words, the message to Laodicea, although harsh, is the result of love. If the church there repents, it will be forgiven.

Verse 20 ("I am standing at the door, knocking . . .") deserves a second look. It has inspired poems, paintings, and stained-glass windows. We usually interpret this verse as a personal invitation for the individual Christian to open the door of the soul to Christ, and as a promise of inner fellowship with him. Yet it most likely refers to communion, in which Christ offers to come and dine with the church. If that is the case, it is one more harsh statement in this message to the church in Laodicea. When that church gathers for communion, Christ is standing outside, knocking at the door! The call to open the door means that in the very central act of the church's worship, Christ has been left out!

Having read and studied the messages to these seven churches, the main question we must ponder is, what kind of message would Christ send today to our churches? Would we be praised for our care of orthodoxy but rebuked for our lack of love, like the Ephesians, or would we be praised for our love but censured for our permissiveness and willingness to compromise, like the Thyatirans? Would we receive only praise and comfort for the difficulties we are about to face, like those early Christians in Smyrna? Would we be told that, although others treat us as outsiders, we shall in fact be insiders, like the Christians in Philadelphia? Or would we be told that we have fallen asleep, that we are "coasting," that very few among us keep to our baptismal vows, like those in Sardis? Worst of all, would we be told that, although we presume to be rich, to have all kinds of resources, to need no one, like the Laodiceans, we in fact are wretched and naked, like lukewarm water fit only to be spit out? The question is worth pondering.

As we finish studying these seven messages to seven churches, we must remember that the rest of the book is also addressed to these same churches. As one commentary reminds us,

> The messages to the Churches are vitally important for a proper understanding of Revelation. While John seems to have his eyes fixed on heavenly realities, his feet are, all the while, firmly on the ground. The communities to and for whom he writes are communities of real men and women, of people who are coping, not always effectively, with difficult and painful situations. (Harrington, *Revelation*, 76)

With that in mind, and without forgetting either those seven concrete churches or the specific churches to which we belong today, let us accompany John in his terrifying and glorious visions.

3. Worship in Heaven
Revelation 4:1–5:14

The setting of the first three chapters was on earth. John was on Patmos, where Christ came to him in a vision and instructed him to write to the seven churches. Now the scene shifts, and John is transported to heaven. From this point on, most of the action will take place in heaven—although with direct connection with what is taking place on earth. What John will see there is also part of what he is to "write in a book . . . and send to the seven churches" (1:11).

As an introduction to this heavenly vision, John describes the worship that takes place in heaven. First he concentrates on the worship that surrounds the throne of God (chap. 4) and then on the Lamb, who is also worthy of worship (chap. 5).

WORSHIP AROUND THE THRONE
Revelation 4:1–11

4:1 **After this I looked, and there in heaven a door stood open! And the first voice, which I had heard speaking to me like a trumpet, said, "Come up here, and I will show you what must take place after this." ² At once I was in the spirit, and there in heaven stood a throne, with one seated on the throne! ³ And the one seated there looks like jasper and carnelian, and around the throne is a rainbow that looks like an emerald. ⁴ Around the throne are twenty-four thrones, and seated on the thrones are twenty-four elders, dressed in white robes, with golden crowns on their heads. ⁵ Coming from the throne are flashes of lightning, and rumblings and peals of thunder, and in front of the throne burn seven flaming torches, which are the seven spirits of God; ⁶ and in front of the throne there is something like a sea of glass, like crystal.**

Around the throne, and on each side of the throne, are four living creatures, full of eyes in front and behind: ⁷ the first living creature like a lion,

the second living creature like an ox, the third living creature with a face like a human face, and the fourth living creature like a flying eagle. [8] And the four living creatures, each of them with six wings, are full of eyes all around and inside. Day and night without ceasing they sing,

"Holy, holy, holy,
the Lord God the Almighty,
who was and is and is to come."

[9] And whenever the living creatures give glory and honor and thanks to the one who is seated on the throne, who lives forever and ever, [10] the twenty-four elders fall before the one who is seated on the throne and worship the one who lives forever and ever; they cast their crowns before the throne, singing,

[11] "You are worthy, our Lord and God,
to receive glory and honor and power,
for you created all things,
and by your will they existed and were created."

The passage begins with a change of venue. The prophet is surprised to see an open door to heaven and hears again the voice he heard in his first vision (1:10), which now invites him to heaven: "Come up here, and I will show you what must take place after this." Here again, as on the previous occasion (1:19), this refers to the suffering the church must endure and to the great struggle leading to God's final triumph. The emphasis here, however, is on how those events on earth relate to what will take place in heaven.

"At once I was in the Spirit," says the prophet—by which he means that he was not transported bodily to heaven but rather in a vision, in a trance. What he sees there is reminiscent of the initial vision of Ezekiel (see Ezekiel 1). But while Ezekiel moves from the edges to the center, finally focusing on the throne of God, John's vision is first and foremost of the throne "and the one seated there."

This One is clearly God. In 7:11, this is made clear when we are told that the multitude "fell on their faces before the throne and worshiped God." John, however, has a very strong sense of the divine majesty and therefore refuses to describe the One seated on the throne. Rather, he gives us glimpses of God's glory, "like jasper and carnelian," and then softens the imagery with a reference to "a rainbow"—which would immediately remind his readers of the covenant with Noah and of the promise of God's watchful eye even in the midst of the storm.

From the throne, John turns his gaze to those surrounding it. There are twenty-four other thrones—presumably smaller ones—and on them sit an equal number of elders with crowns and white robes of victory. Still, the throne of God is at the center of attention, for from it come flashes and peals of thunder, which remind us of God's revelation on Mount Sinai (Ex. 19:16). Here again, as in 1:4, the "seven spirits" probably refer to the sevenfold Spirit of God—although some interpreters believe that they are the seven angels that according to Jewish tradition were God's most immediate servants. According to the most common—and most probable—interpretation, the twenty-four elders represent the people of God who are Israel (the twelve tribes) and the church (the twelve apostles).

The glassy sea in front of the throne probably is not intended to invoke an image of calm, as it would for us today. In ancient times clear glass was almost impossible to produce, much less in large pieces. Therefore, this image would have the same awe-inspiring impact as the references to jasper, carnelian, lightning, and thunder. Furthermore, throughout Revelation the sea is seen most often as a place of chaos and evil that will eventually disappear (21:1: "and the sea was no more"). Most likely, this glassy sea is the same as the "sea of glass mixed with fire" that separates those who conquer from the rest (15:2).

The "four living creatures, full of eyes" are reminiscent of Ezekiel's vision (Ezek. 1:18). (They are not exactly the same, however. In Ezekiel each of the creatures has four faces: those of a human being, a lion, an ox, and an eagle. In Revelation one creature is like a lion, another like an ox, and so on.) These four living creatures probably represent all living beings, for there was a rabbinic tradition that the greatest of wild animals was the lion, the greatest of domestic animals was the ox, the greatest of birds was the eagle, and the greatest of all was the human creature. Thus, the four living creatures bring to the throne the worship of the entire creation.

Here the model for John's vision shifts from Ezekiel 1 to Isaiah 6:2–3, where the prophet says that he saw seraphs attending upon God, each with six wings, and their shouts of acclamation to one another were very similar to what they sing in Revelation: "Holy, holy, holy, is the Lord of hosts; the whole earth is full of his glory."

At this point, there is a heavenly antiphony, for the singing of the four living creatures prompts a response from the twenty-four elders, who "fall down before the one who is seated on the throne and worship" and "cast their crowns before the throne," singing a hymn that glorifies God for having willed and created all things.

There are clear political connotations to this scene of the twenty-four elders casting their crowns. When Tiridates, a king from that area, wished to show his obeisance to Roman Emperor Nero, he did so by placing his crown at Nero's feet. And, if what Roman historian Suetonius wrote is true, that Emperor Domitian did in fact demand to be called *dominus et deus*—"lord and god"—then there is a clear response to that in the hymns of the elders: "You are worthy, our Lord and God." In any case, what the passage says is that all human courts are nothing when compared to the heavenly court and that the one true ruler of all is the One who sits on the heavenly throne—certainly not those who sit on earthly, ephemeral thrones.

Perhaps this entire passage would sound less strange to us, and more familiar, if we remember the hymn we sing so often, inspired precisely on this passage:

> Holy, holy, holy! All the saints adore Thee,
> Casting down their golden crowns around the glassy sea;
> Cherubim and seraphim falling down before Thee,
> Who wert, and art, and evermore shalt be.
> (*The Presbyterian Hymnal*, No. 138)

We begin to realize its impact upon its first readers as we consider the following:

> To the little churches of Asia Minor, this ceaseless worship illuminates the scene that is just behind the scenes of the history they are experiencing. No matter what appears to be the case on earth, God the Creator exists and knows all. The point of the universe is not power but worship. Do not bow before idols or earthly powers, but like heaven's awesome creatures, worship God. (Conn, *Revelation*, 61)

THE BOOK AND THE LAMB
Revelation 5:1–14

5:1 **Then I saw in the right hand of the one seated on the throne a scroll written on the inside and on the back, sealed with seven seals; 2 and I saw a mighty angel proclaiming with a loud voice, "Who is worthy to open the scroll and break its seals?" 3 And no one in heaven or on earth or under the earth was able to open the scroll or to look into it. 4 And I began to weep bitterly because no one was found worthy to open the scroll or to look into it. 5 Then one of the elders said to me, "Do not weep. See, the Lion of the tribe of Judah, the Root of David, has conquered, so that he can open the scroll and its seven seals."**

⁶ Then I saw between the throne and the four living creatures and among the elders a Lamb standing as if it had been slaughtered, having seven horns and seven eyes, which are the seven spirits of God sent out into all the earth. ⁷ He went and took the scroll from the right hand of the one who was seated on the throne. ⁸ When he had taken the scroll, the four living creatures and the twenty-four elders fell before the Lamb, each holding a harp and golden bowls full of incense, which are the prayers of the saints. ⁹ They sing a new song:
> "You are worthy to take the scroll
>   and to open its seals,
>   for you were slaughtered and by your blood you ransomed for God
>   saints from every tribe and language and people and nation;
>   ¹⁰ you have made them to be a kingdom and priests serving our God,
>   and they will reign on earth."

¹¹ Then I looked, and I heard the voice of many angels surrounding the throne and the living creatures and the elders; they numbered myriads of myriads and thousands of thousands, ¹² singing with full voice,
> "Worthy is the Lamb that was slaughtered
> to receive power and wealth and wisdom and might
> and honor and glory and blessing!"

¹³ Then I heard every creature in heaven and on earth and under the earth and in the sea, and all that is in them, singing,
> "To the one seated on the throne and to the Lamb
> be blessing and honor and glory and might
> forever and ever!"

¹⁴ And the four living creatures said, "Amen!" And the elders fell down and worshiped.

The throne-room vision continues. But now attention shifts to a "scroll" in the right hand of God, "written on the inside and on the back, sealed with seven seals." Although the traditional translation is "scroll," and the NRSV follows that tradition, what the Greek actually says is "book," without specifying that it is a scroll.

Most likely, what the vision entails is a fan-folded book. (For some specific purposes, officials customarily would write documents in such fan-folded books.) Two pages of writing could then be sealed facing each other, with the witness's seal and signature on the outside. Thus, if one of the seals was broken, part of the document could be read, but not the rest. This type of document would seem to fit with what follows in Revelation, where at the opening of each seal a part of what is written on the book is unveiled. The "seven" seals are then a sign of fullness, for seven is a perfect number. Also, we know of cases where Roman law required that a will carry seven seals. Thus, a reader from that time would understand that what is written on the book is the eternal and full will of God for creation.

As we read on in Revelation, we will see that what is written is not just a matter of information. The opening of the book is the unfolding of the plan itself. That is why, as we see in verses 2 and 3, it was so difficult to find someone "worthy" to open the book. The breaking of the seals in heaven will set things in motion on earth, and at first no one is found who can do that. That is why John weeps bitterly. He does so not because of frustrated curiosity, but because he realizes that without someone to open the seals, God's plan will not move forward.

The elders, however, seem to know better, and one of them tells John not to weep, for there is someone who can open the book: the "Lion of the tribe of Judah" (a reference to Genesis 49:9–10) and the "Root of David" (a reference to Isaiah 11:1–10). Both of these were common messianic titles at the time, indicating the power of the Messiah and his authority to sit on the throne of David.

John looks, and what does he see? "A Lamb standing as if it had been slaughtered." The Lion of the tribe of Judah is a lamb! Commenting on this passage, New Testament scholar Eugene M. Boring writes:

> John looks at the appointed place in the vision where the Lion was supposed to appear, and what he sees is a slaughtered lamb. Although readers of the Bible may have become so accustomed to it that the effect is lost to us, this is perhaps the most mind-wrenching "rebirth of images" in literature. The slot in the system reserved for the Lion has been filled by the Lamb of God. (Boring, *Revelation*, 108)

To which Dominican scholar Wilfrid J. Harrington adds:

> In his vision John looked for the emergence of a Lion, and saw a slaughtered Lamb! What he learned, and what he tells his readers, is that the Lion *is* the Lamb: the ultimate power of God (Lion) is manifest on the Cross (Lamb). This is why "Lamb" is John's definitive name for Christ. (Harrington, *Revelation*, 87)

The Lamb has seven horns and seven eyes. That does not mean that it is monstrous or deformed. Horns were a symbol of power, and therefore seven horns indicate the plentitude of power. Eyes were a symbol of wisdom, and therefore seven eyes (or seven spirits of God sent throughout the world) indicate that the Lamb also has fullness of knowledge. With this imagery, John is setting up what the rest of the chapter will demonstrate—that the Lamb is worthy of worship jointly with the One who sits on the throne.

The Lamb takes the book directly from the hand of the One who sits on the throne. Thus, if the book is God's plan for creation, that plan is now in the hands of the Lamb. At the point of this transferal of power, heaven breaks forth in a liturgy of praise to the Lamb. That liturgy evolves into a crescendo of three hymns to the Lamb.

First it is the "four living creatures" and the "twenty-four elders" who fall before the Lamb in worship. Significantly, each of the elders holds not only a harp but also a "bowl full of incense, which are the prayers of the saints." In other words, the worship that takes place on earth rises up to heaven and joins the heavenly worship—an important point for the besieged Christians in the seven churches in Asia.

The hymn of the four creatures and the twenty-four elders declares that the Lamb is worthy because it was slaughtered and because through that sacrifice it has ransomed "saints from every tribe and language and people and nation" and made them "a kingdom of priests." The reference here is to the lamb that was slaughtered in Egypt, whose blood was used to seal the doorposts and lintels of Israelite homes so they would be protected from the destruction to be wrought upon the Egyptians (Ex. 12:1–13). That is why "the blood of the Lamb" plays such an important role in Revelation (see 7:14 and 12:11) and in later Christian hymnody.

The initial choir is then joined by "myriads of myriads and thousands of thousands"—in other words, by a countless multitude of angels, who declare the Lamb worthy to receive: power, wealth, wisdom, might, honor, glory, and blessing. Once again, seven is represented, indicating fullness.

All of creation joins in the mighty song. This includes not only every creature in heaven and on earth but also in those two dreaded places, "under the earth"—Hades, the place of the dead—and "in the sea"—the sign of primal chaos. They all join in a song whose most striking feature is that its worship is addressed jointly and equally "to the one seated on the throne and to the Lamb."

This is an important point in Revelation: The Lamb is worthy of praise and honor, and the Lamb holds all power over history—the book with seven seals. It is important because John expects his beloved churches in Asia to face increased pressure and persecution. They will live under the sign and even the reality of the cross. They will need to be reminded that the Lamb who was slain is the One who ultimately holds all power, not only over the church but also over society and even the seemingly powerful empire. To worship the Lamb is to be attuned with the worship that takes place in heaven and with the ultimate goal of all creation, "in heaven, and on earth and under the earth, and in the sea." The ultimate power does not belong to those who now look like lions but to the Lamb who was slaughtered and to those sealed with its blood, who "will reign on earth" (5:10).

4. The First Six Seals
Revelation 6:1–7:17

The stage is now set for the grand drama of history to unfold before John's eyes. As each of the seals is broken in turn, events unfold in heaven that have a great bearing on earth. Many of these events are not pleasant, but in John's vision they are part of the process that ultimately leads to the final victory of the Lamb and of those who belong to the Lamb.

The seven seals will be opened in order, but they will not all take the same space in John's book. The first five will be rather brief, the sixth somewhat longer, and the seventh long enough to merit a separate chapter in this book.

THE FIRST SEAL
Revelation 6:1–2

> 6:1 Then I saw the Lamb open one of the seven seals, and I heard one of the four living creatures call out, as with a voice of thunder, "Come!" 2 I looked, and there was a white horse! Its rider had a bow; a crown was given to him, and he came out conquering and to conquer.

The first four seals form a unit and parallel each other. Together, they tell of what has come to be known as "the four horsemen of the Apocalypse." As each of the seals is opened, one of the four living creatures that we met in 4:6 calls out, "Come!" At this beckoning, a horse comes out, each of a different color and with a rider having particular attributes. It is significant that the common word for "rider" is not used here, but rather the unusual wording "the one sitting on it." These are exactly the same words used to refer to God as "the one sitting on the throne." Thus, the purpose of these words may be to depict these four horses as false seats of power—false thrones, so to speak, that seem to have ultimate power but do not. They are still subject to the One who sits on the real throne.

The first horse is white. Since in 19:11 there is a white horse whose "rider is called Faithful and True," some interpreters have thought that this first horse is a positive figure and that it represents the preaching of the gospel. But given the context here, this horse and its rider must be seen to be part of the group of four that bring suffering upon the earth.

This first rider is armed with a bow. The Parthians, who had built a vast empire just east of the Roman borders and who had become Rome's traditional enemy in the region, were noted for their mounted archers—most other armies used archers as infantry. Therefore, to a reader in Asia Minor in the first century, the image of a rider with a bow would immediately have brought to mind thoughts of a Parthian invasion. That is probably what is meant by this horse and its rider. The horse is white, the color of victory. To the rider "was given" a crown—actually, a wreath of victory.

This sort of passive construction was common in Jewish literature, when an action was attributed to God as a way to avoid mentioning God's name. Thus, the original readers would have understood that God had given victory to the Parthians, Rome's hated enemy, and that foreign invasion, destructive though it might be, was not beyond God's control. (The phrase that the NRSV translates as "conquering and to conquer" probably reflects a Hebrew idiom meaning "continuously conquering.")

THE SECOND SEAL
Revelation 6:3–4

> 6:3 **When he opened the second seal, I heard the second living creature call out, "Come!"** [4] **And out came another horse, bright red; its rider was permitted to take peace from the earth, so that people would slaughter one another; and he was given a great sword.**

As in the previous case, the Lamb opens a seal, a living creature calls, and out comes a horse. In this case the horse is "bright red"—actually, "fiery red." Its rider is given a "great sword." Two different words in Revelation are translated as "sword." Here, the NRSV correctly says "great sword" to indicate that this was a particular type of sword that symbolized power and authority. (There is another Greek word for another type of sword, which we shall find in connection with the fourth rider [6:8] and was also the type of sword coming out of Christ's mouth in 1:16.) What this second rider carries is the heavy sword that was used for swinging and cutting rather than for stabbing. It was also a symbol of imperial authority—in particular, the emperor's authority to decree the death penalty, which was called "the right of the sword" and which could also be exercised by provincial governors. Thus, after the first rider made original readers of this book think of Parthia and foreign invasion, they would see in the second rider a symbol of Rome and its power.

Ironically, Rome boasted of having brought peace to the lands it had conquered—the *pax romana*. This is partially true. But it is also true that many of the conquered people were recruited as Roman auxiliaries to fight against their former neighbors. Constant rebellions plagued the Roman Empire. For many of the conquered peoples, the much-vaunted Roman peace was the peace of death. It is also clear that John the Seer had neither love nor admiration for the Roman Empire. Thus, in an ironic twist of the Roman claim to have brought peace, John says that this rider "was permitted [again, by God] to take peace from the earth, so that people would slaughter one another."

THE THIRD SEAL
Revelation 6:5–6

> 6:5 **When he opened the third seal, I heard the third living creature call out, "Come!" I looked, and there was a black horse! Its rider held a pair of scales in his hand,** 6 **and I heard what seemed to be a voice in the midst of the four living creatures saying, "A quart of wheat for a day's pay, and three quarts of barley for a day's pay, but do not damage the olive oil and the wine!"**

The opening of the third seal is parallel to the previous two. This time the horse is black, and its rider carries "a pair of scales." Scales are the sign of trade. Again, the rich boasted of how the trade that was now possible had improved conditions for everybody. But that was not always the case for the poor, as was clear in the province of Asia.

That province was one of the richest of the empire. Its land was fertile, and its many seaports and rivers made for ease in trade. After the area had been incorporated into the Roman Empire, many wealthy landowners—both local and foreign—discovered that they could make much more money on the same acreage by devoting the land to vineyards and olive groves rather than to grains. As their business ventures succeeded, they bought more land, which in turn was converted also to olives and vines.

The result was great wealth for the landowners and food scarcity for the lower echelons of the population. Since this was happening in several provinces, in A.D. 92 Emperor Domitian issued a decree ordering that the vineyards in all provinces must be reduced by half. Apparently there were also attempts to prohibit the planting of new olive groves. But the landed aristocracy—especially in Asia—raised such a protest that Domitian was forced to rescind his edict. The result was rising prices for grain and increased famine among the populace.

That is the context for the cry that comes from an unspecified source in the midst of the four living creatures: "A quart of wheat for a day's pay, and three quarts of barley for a day's pay, but do not damage the olive oil and the wine!" What the NRSV translates as "a day's pay" is actually a *denarius*, a coin that was the traditional wage for a day. Normally, a denarius would have bought 12 quarts of wheat or 24 quarts of barley—a grain that was considered of lesser quality. Thus, what the unidentified source is voicing is an ironic protest against a system of trade that produced an inflationary rate of 1,200 percent in the price of wheat and 800 percent in the case of barley. The third rider represents famine, caused not simply by food shortages but rather by a destructive system of trade—one that sits on its horse as upon the throne of God.

THE FOURTH SEAL
Revelation 6:7–8

> 6:7 **When he opened the fourth seal, I heard the voice of the fourth living creature call out, "Come!"** [8] **I looked and there was a pale green horse! Its rider's name was Death, and Hades followed with him; they were given authority over a fourth of the earth, to kill with sword, famine, and pestilence, and by the wild animals of the earth.**

The fourth rider, introduced in the same manner as the previous three, epitomizes all of them. Its horse is "pale"—a better translation would be "greenish," like a corpse in the early stages of corruption. This is the only rider who is given a name: "Death." He is accompanied by "Hades," the traditional name for the underworld where the dead were kept. As the other three riders—foreign invasion, domestic injustice and turmoil, and unjust trade—are let loose upon the earth, the result is that Death and Hades are also released.

The sentence that begins "they were given authority" may refer either

to Death and Hades or to all four riders. Since this is the end of this series of riders, this section is best understood as a summary: The four riders were given authority (again, by God, who never loses control) over a
fourth of the earth, to kill in various manners. (The "sword" mentioned
here is the shorter sword used for stabbing and does not have the symbolic
connotations of the "sword" in 6:4.)

Much has been written about "the four horsemen of the Apocalypse"
and when they will come. Pastor Amanda J. Burr, in a sermon on this
topic, comments most appropriately:

> Although John saw the horses and horsemen arriving at any moment in his
> time, we try to figure out when they will come in our time, as if they had
> not yet arrived. I believe the truth to be that they have already been here,
> that they are here now, and that they are coming again. The four horsemen
> of the Apocalypse ride among us, confronting us every day of the world.
> Thus is this text relevant for today, not as a book of secret prophecies that
> can only be decoded by a select group of alarmist paranoids, but as a con-
> stant reminder that the Divine is attentive to what we do and how we are
> with one another. (Rogers and Jeter, *Preaching through the Apocalypse*, 92)

THE FIFTH SEAL
Revelation 6:9–11

> 6:9 When he opened the fifth seal, I saw under the altar the souls of those
> who had been slaughtered for the word of God and for the testimony they
> had given; [10] they cried out with a loud voice, "Sovereign Lord, holy and
> true, how long will it be before you judge and avenge our blood on the in-
> habitants of the earth?" [11] They were each given a white robe and told to
> rest a little longer, until the number would be complete both of their fellow
> servants and of their brothers and sisters, who were soon to be killed as they
> themselves had been killed.

The fifth seal surprises us by its unexpected content. It shows us another
inexplicable calamity, namely, that so many through the ages have suffered
"for the word of God and for the testimony" they have given. In this vision,
they are "under the altar" because there was a common thought that, just
as the blood of sacrificed animals ended up under the altar, so did the souls
of those sacrificed for God await the resurrection under the altar.

These souls of martyrs past are now revealed to be awaiting their final
resurrection and crying for justice. The answer, which was already found
in Jewish apocalyptic literature, is that they must wait until their ap-

pointed number is complete. This probably should not be read in the literal sense that there is a fixed number of martyrs required before the end will come. If we remember that the book is addressed to Christians facing potential prosecution and death, what they are being told is that they may be added to the company of martyrs and that their own sacrifice would be a contribution to the glorious end when they will all rise in glory and God shall "judge and avenge [their] blood." Meanwhile, those who suffered death for their faith already have the white robes of victory, even while they await the final outcome of history.

THE SIXTH SEAL
Revelation 6:12–7:17

The Opening of the Seal (6:12–17)

6:12 **When he opened the sixth seal, I looked, and there came a great earthquake; the sun became black as sackcloth, the full moon became like blood,** [13] **and the stars of the sky fell to the earth as the fig tree drops its winter fruit when shaken by a gale.** [14] **The sky vanished like a scroll rolling itself up, and every mountain and island was removed from its place.** [15] **Then the kings of the earth and the magnates and the generals and the rich and the powerful, and everyone, slave and free, hid in the caves and among the rocks of the mountains,** [16] **calling to the mountains and rocks, "Fall on us and hide us from the face of the one seated on the throne and from the wrath of the Lamb;** [17] **for the great day of their wrath has come, and who is able to stand?"**

In some ways, the sixth seal is a response to the cries of the martyrs in the fifth seal. The awaited hour now approaches, and its coming is marked by a series of catastrophes of cosmic proportions. The four riders symbolized evils and destruction brought about by human agency. The destruction here is much greater and is described in poetic imagery that is mostly borrowed from the Old Testament. Here again, as throughout the book, the number seven appears, for there are seven events listed:

1. there is a great earthquake
2. the sun darkens
3. the full moon becomes like blood
4. the stars fall from the sky ("as the fig tree drops its winter fruit when shaken by a gale"—a beautiful image!)
5. the sky vanishes ("like a scroll rolling itself up")

6. the mountains and islands are removed
7. the people feel great consternation

Seven classes of people feel this great consternation—with the emphasis falling on the powerful to make it clear that not even the mightiest will escape:

1. kings of the earth
2. magnates
3. generals
4. the rich
5. the powerful
6. the slave
7. the free

This double set of sevens shows that the destruction is total. Nothing remains in place, and no one is high enough or low enough to escape.

The consternation is such that people run into caves, not so much to save their lives as to escape "from the face of the one seated on the throne and from the wrath of the Lamb." The wrath of the Lamb! Once again, John's vision turns things upside down. Earlier, when looking for a lion, he sees a lamb. Now, all these people, many of whom would appear as lions of society—kings, magnates, generals—are hiding from the wrath of a lamb!

To us, who have a significant investment in our society and whom the present order rewards with relative comfort and security, all of this may sound unbearably negative. Not so to John's first readers, who may well have thought of brother Antipas (2:13) as one of those whose souls await the consummation under the altar and who also had to face the possibility of a similar fate. In our competitive society, many of us, though calling ourselves followers of the Lamb, eagerly try to make a place for ourselves like lions. To act like a lamb is unnatural and even cowardly. We laugh at such people! And yet, says John, power belongs to the Lamb, and one day even the most powerful kings will have to answer to the wrath of the Lamb. Farfetched? The imagery, perhaps, but not the reality! As John wrote, "Let anyone who has an ear listen to what the Spirit is saying to the churches" (2:7).

The Sealed from Israel (7:1–8)

7:1 **After this I saw four angels standing at the four corners of the earth, holding back the four winds of the earth so that no wind could blow on earth** or sea or against any tree. ² I saw another angel ascending from the rising of the sun, having the seal of the living God, and he called with a loud voice to the four angels who had been given power to damage earth and sea, ³ saying, "Do not damage the earth or the sea or the trees, until we have marked the servants of our God with a seal on their foreheads."

⁴ And I heard the number of those who were sealed, one hundred forty-four thousand, sealed out of every tribe of the people of Israel:

⁵ From the tribe of Judah twelve thousand sealed,
from the tribe of Reuben twelve thousand,
from the tribe of Gad twelve thousand,
⁶ from the tribe of Asher twelve thousand,
from the tribe of Naphtali twelve thousand,
from the tribe of Manasseh twelve thousand,
⁷ from the tribe of Simeon twelve thousand,
from the tribe of Levi twelve thousand,
from the tribe of Issachar twelve thousand,
⁸ from the tribe of Zebulun twelve thousand,
from the tribe of Joseph twelve thousand,
from the tribe of Benjamin twelve thousand sealed.

Clearly, this passage cannot be taken as part of a chronology of the end times. In Revelation 6 there was a great earthquake, so that even the mountains disappeared. Now we are told that the four angels of destruction are given the instruction "do not damage the earth or the sea or the trees, until we have marked the servants of our God." It is important to remember this, for the various interpretations of Revelation that turn it into a blueprint for the end of the world are so prevalent in our society that it is difficult to rid ourselves of that presupposition.

The seven seals are not successive stages leading to the end, like periods in world history. Rather, they are images whose purpose is to allow Christians, living under the present tribulations, to live as those who are moving toward God's future, as those sealed by the Lamb. As such, they seek to place the present suffering under the light of the lordship of the Lamb and to indicate that all present systems of lordship, power, and authority are naught before "the wrath of the Lamb," whom those systems ignore and even mock.

In any case, there is a pause in the scenes of destruction we have just been reading. This adds to the dramatic effect of the whole. The first six seals moved in rapid succession. There was increasing destruction and visions ever more imposing. We can hardly wait for the opening of the seventh seal. But John makes us wait!

Behind the opening verses of this chapter stands the ancient worldview, according to which the earth was flat and square, and the four winds that blew from the corners were evil winds. Just as we are ready for the opening of the seventh seal, so are the four evil winds ready to add their share of damage to the evils of war, famine, pestilence, and earthquake. But just as we are bidden to wait, so are the four angels that have control over those winds ordered to wait. The one bringing this order is another angel "having the seal of the living God." The "seal" here reminds us of the "seven seals" of the scroll, but it is much more than that. In ancient times, the king's representative—the head of government, or what today would be the prime minister—held the king's seal. This authorized him to issue orders in the name of the king. Likewise, this angel has the authority to command the other angels because he carries God's seal.

The seal, however, also was used to mark one's property. We have a remnant of that today in the branding of cattle. In ancient times, this was often done in the case of slaves. Notice that in verse 3 we are told that the delay in the destructive power of the four winds is to give time "until we have marked the servants of our God with a seal on their foreheads." The word that the NRSV translates as "servants" also means "slaves." Thus, the meaning is that those to be sealed are to be marked as the possession of God. (Later, we shall come to passages where others are described as being marked with a negative sign—the sign of the beast.)

This entire passage is reminiscent of Ezekiel 9:1–6, where God has decided to destroy the idolaters in Jerusalem, and six "executioners of the city, each with his weapon for slaughter in his hand" are prepared to do the task. But before they do this, God sends a "man clothed in linen" to go through the city "and put a mark on the foreheads" of those who have remained faithful. The difference is that, while in Ezekiel those who are marked are spared the pain of the others, in Revelation the sealing of the saints does not protect them from suffering and death. On the contrary, in many ways they will suffer precisely because they have been sealed. But they certainly will be spared the real, final death, the "second death."

Interpreters have suggested that the use of the term "seal" in this context would have led John's original readers to think of their own baptism, which from a very early time was known as God's "seal" upon the believers. In any case, the notion that God's faithful are "sealed" was quite common in New Testament times (see John 6:27; Rom. 4:11; 2 Cor. 1:22; Eph. 1:13; 4:30).

Those who are sealed are 144,000, "out of every tribe of the people of Israel." The number 144,000 has led to much speculation. In reality, there is nothing strange about it. The tribes are twelve. Twelve is also a number of perfection. A thousand means a great multitude. The number 144,000 =

12 × 12 × 1,000. What is meant is a very large number and an absolutely perfect number. Not one person who should have been included is left out—a message of great hope for John's readers, whose tribulations would often make them wonder if God had forgotten them and not counted them among the number to be saved.

The listing of the twelve tribes has some peculiarities. The first thing we note is that instead of listing the tribes in the order of precedence of their patriarchs, the tribe of Judah appears first. This is probably because the Lamb, the "Root of David," is of the tribe of Judah. The tribe of Dan, however, is not listed. Apparently there was a tradition among the Jews of the time (to which early Christian writers refer) that the Antichrist would come from that tribe. Among Christians, it was also said that Judas was from that tribe. For one reason or another, Dan is excluded from the list. To bring the number back up to twelve, Manasseh is included—although in fact Manasseh was part of Joseph.

There is disagreement among interpreters as to whether or not these 144,000 are intended to be understood as the descendants of Israel. Some think that John simply uses these Hebrew names in order to say that the church has taken the place of Israel—that the church is the true Israel and that the old is now rejected. There are, however, too many passages in Revelation that lead us to think that John is convinced of Israel's continued place in the plan of salvation. Remember, for instance, the twenty-four elders (or read 21:12–14, where the holy city has twelve gates, one for each tribe of Israel, and twelve foundations, each for one of the apostles). Therefore, it would seem that the passage we are studying refers to the sealing of a "remnant of Israel"—a fairly common theme in the Old Testament prophets that John, rather than diminishing, has raised to the level of an absolutely perfect and complete number: 144,000.

The Sealed from among the Nations (7:9–17)

7:9 **After this I looked, and there was a great multitude that no one could count, from every nation, from all tribes and peoples and languages, standing before the throne and before the Lamb, robed in white, with palm branches in their hands.** [10] **They cried out in a loud voice, saying,**
> **"Salvation belongs to our God who is seated on the throne, and to the Lamb!"**
[11] **And all the angels stood around the throne and around the elders and the four living creatures, and they fell on their faces before the throne and worshiped God,** [12] **singing,**
> **"Amen! Blessing and glory and wisdom**

and thanksgiving and honor
and power and might
be to our God forever and ever!
    Amen."

¹³ Then one of the elders addressed me, saying, "Who are these, robed in
white, and where have they come from? ¹⁴ I said to him, "Sir, you are the
one that knows." Then he said to me, "These are they who have come out
of the great ordeal; they have washed their robes and made them white in
the blood of the Lamb.

¹⁵ For this reason they are before the throne of God,
        and worship him day and night within his temple,
        and the one who is seated on the throne will shelter them.
¹⁶ They will hunger no more, and thirst no more;
        the sun will not strike them,
        nor any scorching heat;
¹⁷ for the Lamb at the center of the throne will be their
    shepherd,
        and he will guide them to springs of the water of life,
        and God will wipe away every tear from their eyes."

As in the case of the 144,000, scholars are not in agreement as to who con-
stitutes this "multitude." Some believe it should be equated with the
144,000 now seen worshiping in heaven. Even if the 144,000 are actually
Israelites, some argue that the same is true of this multitude and that the
phrase "from every nation, from all tribes and peoples and languages"
should be understood in the sense of these being Hebrews returning from
the various lands to which they had been dispersed.

Most likely, this is a different multitude. These are gentiles "from every
nation, from all tribes and peoples and languages" who are presented as
the counterpart of the 144,000 Hebrews sealed in the previous passage.
Thus, as in the case of the twenty-four elders, or of the twelve gates and
twelve foundations of the Holy City, John is speaking of the people of God
composed of two branches, one from among the descendants of Abraham
and another from among the Gentiles.

The members of this great multitude wear white robes, a symbol of victory and probably another reference to baptism, since from a very early
date it was customary to dress newly baptized Jews, just as they emerged
from the waters, in white robes. The palm branches are also a sign of joy
and victory. Remember, for instance, the reception of Jesus into Jerusalem.
Also, in 1 Maccabees 13:51, we are told that to celebrate their victory the
Jews entered the citadel of Jerusalem "with praise and palm branches." In

later Christian art, a person depicted with a palm branch indicates that the person is a martyr, one who has won the ultimate victory.

What they sing is a formula of praise that appears in the Old Testament (see Psalm 3:8 and John 2:9) but with the all-important addition, "and to the Lamb." To readers steeped in the Hebrew Bible, John clearly is claiming for the Lamb an honor and a worship that traditionally belong only to God.

The angels and the living creatures now join the song of praise. Their initial "Amen" would remind Christians of the manner in which the congregation usually responded to the prayers of the person leading worship. Another antiphonal setting develops in which this heavenly choir sings a hymn that ascribes the following to God: blessing, glory, wisdom, thanksgiving, honor, power, and might.

The question and answer in verses 13 and 14 are didactic in character. The elder obviously knows who these people are and asks only so that John will in turn ask for an explanation. The explanation is that they are the ones "who have come out of the great ordeal" and who have "washed their robes and made them white in the blood of the Lamb." The reference here is to the suffering of Christians under persecution. These are the ones who, as the seven letters said; "have conquered." They have conquered because they were sealed by God—because they were God's own.

But being sealed by God did not keep them from having to go through the ordeal, just as the Lamb also conquered by being slaughtered. "They have washed their robes and made them white in the blood of the Lamb." This apparently contradictory phrase—one does not make robes white by dipping them in blood—is much more than religious formula. It does not mean simply—as we often read it today—that they believed in Jesus and therefore were cleansed by his blood. This phrase means also that they have shared in the sacrifice of the Lamb by themselves being subjected to suffering, having gone through "the great ordeal." Thus, the "seal" of God does not mark believers for protection against evil, but only from being defeated by it. We would do well to ponder these words of one biblical commentator:

> One should keep in mind that, for John, the victors are those who "loved not their lives even unto death" (12:11). The "sealing," assurance of divine concern, will entail no "rapture" for the elect. They will be "caught up" indeed, but caught up in the tribulation, helpless victims—helpless as their Lord on his cross. For them, as for him, there will be no legion of angels. We must look for no miracle, apart from the abiding miracle of God's loving care." (Harrington, *Revelation*, 99)

But not all is negative. In the end, the elder tells John that the beautiful vision depicted in the hymn in verses 15 through 17 will take place. Those who went through the ordeal, who even offered their blood as the Lamb has offered his, will be "before the throne of God," worshiping constantly—that is, rejoicing, for worship of the true God is the human creature's greatest joy.

Those who found no shelter from suffering will now have God for their shelter. (The word used here could also be translated as "tabernacle," thus bringing to mind images of the joyful Feast of Tabernacles.) All their suffering will now be past. "They will hunger no more, and thirst no more." (Again, these are not just poetic images. Remember the scarcity of food in Asia, the inflated prices, and the fact that many of the Christians to whom John was writing were probably quite poor.) The victory will be complete—so complete that even the Lamb that was slaughtered will have become their Shepherd, and the tears from their eyes will be wiped away—as a mother wipes the tears from a child's eyes—by none other than God!

5. The Seventh Seal and the Seven Trumpets
Revelation 8:1–11:19

THE SEVENTH SEAL
Revelation 8:1

> 8:1 **When the Lamb opened the seventh seal, there was silence in heaven for about half an hour.**

There has been much debate as to the meaning of this half hour of silence. Most likely, it refers to a Jewish belief that before God created the world there was silence and that there will also be silence at the end. Thus, this silence announces the beginning of the new creation.

In any case, this is certainly one of the most dramatic moments in the entire book of Revelation—and yet one that we often miss. Imagine this book being read for the first time to a congregation in Thyatira. The tension has been mounting. As each seal is opened, new and more impressive vistas unfold before the eyes of the congregation. Now they come to the final, the seventh, seal! If before they have heard voices like mighty waterfalls, like peals of thunder or like the roar of lions, what are they to hear now? The tension mounts. All are hanging from the words of the reader. And the words are read: "When the Lamb opened the seventh seal, there was silence in heaven for half an hour"! As we imagine that setting, we can almost hear the congregation's startled intake of breath!

What are we to say about this? Perhaps we would do best to say nothing and to respect the silence—to learn that God's time is not our time and to take this as a lesson on what it means to wait on God.

THE FIRST SIX TRUMPETS
Revelation 8:2–9:21

Once again, John tells us of a vision that unfolds in seven steps. And once again, the first steps will pass quite rapidly, only to make us wait all the more eagerly for the seventh while we are told of other visions. The series of trumpets will be interrupted after the sixth, just as the series of seals was interrupted after the sixth. This device, of telling of the first components in a set (seals or trumpets) in a few words and then prolonging the last, is a way of warning John's readers that, no matter how rapidly things may seem to be moving, they have to be ready for the long haul.

In hearing one of their number read out loud about the seven seals and in seeing how rapidly the first four are dealt with, the original recipients of the book would have expected the end to be, so to speak, "around the corner." There were only three more seals. But then the fifth and sixth would take longer. And upon the opening of the seventh seal they would discover that there were now seven trumpets. Once again, the first four trumpets would go rather quickly. But not so for the rest. Eventually those original recipients of the book would discover that beyond the seven seals and the seven trumpets there are seven bowls of wrath!

Thus, in spite of what we have been repeatedly told, John is not telling his contemporaries that the end is coming very soon and that therefore all they have to do is hang on a little longer. Rather, he is telling them that the present, as well as the future, are in God's hand and that therefore the end is worth waiting for and living for.

The Setting of the Scene (8:2–5)

> 8:2 **And I saw the seven angels who stand before God, and seven trumpets were given to them.**
> **3 Another angel with a golden censer came and stood at the altar; he was given a great quantity of incense to offer with the prayers of all the saints on the golden altar that is before the throne. 4 And the smoke of the incense, with the prayers of the saints, rose before God from the hand of the angel. 5 Then the angel took the censer and filled it with fire from the altar and threw it on the earth; and there were peals of thunder, rumblings, flashes of lightning, and an earthquake.**

The "seven angels" are mentioned here for the first time. Some interpreters believe them to be the same as the "seven spirits" of 1:4, 3:1, 4:5, and 5:6. (We are inclined to interpret the term "seven spirits" in another fashion. See the discussion on Revelation 1:4.) The "seven angels of the presence" were a fairly common notion in Jewish literature of the time. They were the principal angels, who stood "in the presence" of God. By joining various texts, interpreters thought that the angels' names were Michael, Gabriel, Raphael, Uriel, Raguel, Sariel, and Remiel. Of these,

only Michael is mentioned by name in Revelation (12:7). (Since in Hebrew the name Gabriel means "God is my strength," there are some interpreters who suggest that the "mighty angel" mentioned in 5:2, 10:1,
and 18:21 is another way of referring to Gabriel.)

These seven angels "were given" seven trumpets. As is repeatedly the
case throughout Revelation, this apparently impersonal use of the passive
voice is an indirect way of saying that God was the subject of the action.
It was God who gave the angels the trumpets, just as in chapter 6 it was
God who gave the riders their power.

Trumpets are the sign of divine presence and intervention. In the Old
Testament, God's presence announces itself with the sound of a mighty
trumpet (Ex. 19:16–19; 20:18). As a result, solemn religious rituals were
also announced with trumpets (Lev. 23:24; 25:9). Combining the two, Israel's praise for God's mighty acts has recourse to the image of a trumpet
sounding: "God has gone up with a shout, the Lord with the sound of a
trumpet" (Psalm 47:5). The trumpet is also a proclamation of divine action (Isa. 18:3; 27:13) and specifically of the "day of the Lord" (Joel 2:1).

In Ezekiel 33:2–6, which may have provided direct inspiration for the
passage we are studying, the image is of a sentinel who "sees the sword
coming upon the land and blows the trumpet and warns the people." If the
people do not heed the warning and take cover, "their blood shall be upon
their own heads." This gives us an indication of the purpose of the trumpets about to be blown. They—and even the destruction that comes with
them—are warnings to bring people to repentance and obedience. Thus,
a scholar who has compared the seven trumpets with the bowls of wrath
that appear later, has concluded that

> in the trumpet visions it is clearly his [John's] intention to show that the
> plagues actually attain only a part (a third) of the affected region. Indeed,
> the plagues do not truly have the character of destructive judgment, but
> rather of a sign that calls to repentance in that it points to God's power over
> the world and history. (Roloff, *Revelation*, 105)

The passage about the angel with the golden censer shows an interesting understanding of the effect of human worship. First of all, "the prayers
of all the saints," meaning the prayers of the church on earth, are joined
with the incense burned at the heavenly altar, and all of it together rises
to the throne of God. Thus, earthly worship joins with heavenly worship
so that, in a sense, the two are one. (Note that even in heaven the "throne
of God" is above the altar. Heavenly worship is still creaturely worship.)
Second, the prayers of the saints, joined with heavenly worship, come back

down to earth. God's wrath answers the prayers of the suffering saints. "The angel took the censer and filled it with fire from the altar and threw it on earth." What from a human point of view might seem sheer disaster ("peals of thunder, rumblings, flashes of lightning, and an earthquake") is the fire of heavenly, true worship thrown down on earth.

This is not to be taken as an explanation for natural disasters. John's question is not, Why do earthquakes happen? Rather, his questions are the following: How are Christians to withstand the pressures of society around them and the prospect of increasing persecution? How are they to view their life of worship? What are they to think of a world and a society around them that seem able to go on their merry way, paying little heed to God's will? Will such people go unpunished? And John's answer to all of them is, Certainly not! Even major disasters, such as earthquakes, are just a warning, a mere sign of the wrath to come!

The First Four Trumpets (8:6–13)

8:6 **Now the seven angels who had the seven trumpets made ready to blow them.**

⁷ **The first angel blew his trumpet, and there came hail and fire, mixed with blood, and they were hurled to the earth; and a third of the earth was burned up, and a third of the trees were burned up, and all green grass was burned up.**

⁸ **The second angel blew his trumpet, and something like a great mountain, burning with fire, was thrown into the sea. ⁹ A third of the sea became blood, a third of the living creatures in the sea died, and a third of the ships were destroyed.**

¹⁰ **The third angel blew his trumpet, and a great star fell from heaven, blazing like a torch, and it fell on a third of the rivers and on the springs of water. ¹¹ The name of the star is Wormwood. A third of the waters became wormwood, and many died from the water, because it was made bitter.**

¹² **The fourth angel blew his trumpet, and a third of the sun was struck, and a third of the moon, and a third of the stars, so that a third of their light was darkened; a third of the day was kept from shining, and likewise the night.**

¹³ **Then I looked, and I heard an eagle crying with a loud voice as it flew in midheaven. "Woe, woe, woe to the inhabitants of the earth, at the blasts of the other trumpets that the three angels are about to blow!"**

As has been said above, the purpose of the evils that will be let loose upon the earth is not the cruel vindictiveness of a God who rejoices over suffering. The purpose, rather, is to call the world to repentance. That is why the destructive power of all these plagues is limited to a portion of the whole. Note, however, that whereas the rider that was let loose at the opening of the fourth seal was given power over a fourth of the earth, now most of the evils unleashed by the angels with the first four trumpets destroy one-third of the whole. The warning is being given in a crescendo of woe and destruction.

The calamities that follow the first five trumpets—as well as those brought about by the bowls of wrath in Revelation 16—are reminiscent of the plagues of Egypt, although they are not a mere repetition. Jewish readers—or Gentiles steeped in the Hebrew scriptures—would immediately think of the mighty acts of God in freeing the children of Israel from the bondage of Egypt. But they would see that John is speaking of even mightier events. This connection with Egypt is significant, for it means that Revelation compares the Roman Empire and its existing political situation not only to the Babylonian exile but also to the captivity of Israel in Egypt. As the fall of Babylon put an end to the Babylonian exile, so does Revelation announce the fall of the new Babylon; and as the plagues put an end to bondage in Egypt, so does Revelation announce new and worse plagues upon the existing order of oppression and injustice.

As the first angel blows his trumpet, the "hail and fire, mixed with blood" remind us of the seventh plague in Egypt (Ex. 9:23–26). In Exodus, however, the hail destroys "everything that was in the open field" as well as "all the plants" and "every tree." Here, the most destructive element is fire, which burns up a third of the earth and a third of the trees but "all the green grass." Once again John surprises us with small touches of the unexpected. Throughout this passage, almost everything will be destroyed in thirds. But the grass is completely destroyed. Perhaps the grass is treated differently because it readily grows back in one season. Such unexpected details would awaken the interest of a congregation hearing this writing and would remind them that God is always free to do the unexpected.

The second and third trumpets remind us of the first plague of Egypt (see Ex. 7:19–21). The similarities, as well as the differences, are interesting. In Egypt the plague is brought about by Aaron striking the waters with his staff. Here the origin of the plague is much more dramatic: a burning mountain and a flaming star, both falling from the sky. In Egypt all the waters—including even that held in vats and reservoirs—turned to blood; here a third of all the waters become contaminated. In Egypt the plague is limited to the waters of Egypt; here the vision is of a worldwide phenomenon. Thus, whereas in Exodus those who resisted God were Pharaoh and his followers, here those who resist God are the vast majority of humankind throughout the world.

The star falling from heaven is named "Wormwood," and it turns the waters into wormwood. In contrast with Exodus, where a single plague strikes all the waters of Egypt, turning them into blood, here a first plague turns the sea into blood, and a second turns the fresh water into wormwood. "Wormwood" is a bitter herb from which absinthe is extracted. It is not only bitter but poisonous, to the point that other plants near it often wither and die. Thus the phrase "many died from it, because it was bitter" means more than that they simply could not stand the taste. The water was bitter because it had been poisoned.

Those who are inclined to interpret the book of Revelation too literally and not realize that much of its power is precisely in its metaphoric imagery should note that a single flaming star falls on a third of all the rivers and springs of water. Physically and literally, it is difficult to envision how a single star could fall in so many places. If read as poetic metaphor, the image is powerful. If read as astronomic description, it is simply baffling.

When the fourth angel blows his trumpet, the plagues reach the sky itself. Note that the plague unleashed by the first angel had to do with the earth, and the destructions released by the second and third affected the sea and the waters. Now we turn to the sky. Thus, nothing is left untouched—neither land, nor sea, nor even the sun and the stars. This new disaster is parallel to the ninth plague of Egypt (see Ex. 10:21–23), where Moses stretched his hand toward heaven, and there was darkness in all the land—except where the Israelites lived—for three days. Here, however, the darkness is more dramatic, for it is caused by the partial extinguishing of the luminaries themselves. In another of those interesting reminiscences in reverse, whereas in Egypt the plague lasted three days, here it attains one-third of all the celestial bodies. The phrase "a third of the day was kept from shining, and likewise the night" does not mean that they were shortened but rather that they were darkened.

By the end of this fourth trumpet, it appears that all of creation—earth, sea, and sky—has been struck by disaster. But there is much more to come. An eagle (or, perhaps in a better translation, a vulture) cries "woe" thrice, seeming to indicate that each of the three pending trumpets will bring even greater suffering than the previous four.

The Fifth Trumpet
and the First Woe (9:1–12)

9:1 **And the fifth angel blew his trumpet, and I saw a star that had fallen from heaven to earth, and he was given the key to the shaft of the bottom-**

less pit; ² he opened the shaft of the bottomless pit, and from the shaft rose smoke like the smoke of a great furnace, and the sun and the air was darkened with the smoke from the shaft. ³ Then from the smoke came locusts on the earth, and they were given authority like the authority of scorpions of the earth. ⁴ They were told not to damage the grass of the earth or any green growth or any tree, but only those people who do not have the seal of God on their foreheads. ⁵ They were allowed to torture them for five months, but not to kill them, and their torture was like the torture of a scorpion when it stings someone. ⁶ And in those days people will seek death but will not find it; they will long to die, but death will flee from them.

⁷ In appearance the locusts were like horses equipped for battle. On their heads were what looked like crowns of gold; their faces were like human faces, ⁸ their hair like women's hair, and their teeth like lions' teeth; ⁹ they had scales like iron breastplates, and the noise of their wings was like the noise of many chariots with horses rushing into battle. ¹⁰ They have tails like scorpions, with stingers, and in their tails is their power to harm people for five months. ¹¹ They have as king over them the angel of the bottomless pit; his name in Hebrew is Abaddon, and in Greek he is called Apollyon.

¹² The first woe has passed. There are still two woes to come.

The fifth trumpet reminds us of the eighth plague of Egypt (Ex. 10:12–19), when locusts invaded the land. But, once again, this newer version of the plague is worse than the former. In Egypt the locusts ate whatever vegetation was left, but here they will be instructed not to attack the vegetation but only "those people who do not have the seal of God on their foreheads." Their purpose is not to kill these people but only to torment them by stinging them like scorpions. The pain will be such that "in those days people will seek death but will not find it; they will long to die, but death will flee from them." The "five months" that this plague will last are probably a reference to the life span of a locust (therefore, the life span of a swarm of locusts).

Verses 7 through 11 describe the locusts unleashed by this fifth trumpet. In this description there are also echoes of Joel 1:6–2:11, where the prophet describes a plague of locusts as if it were a foreign invasion. According to Joel, this enemy is "powerful and innumerable, its teeth are lions' teeth, and it has the fangs of a lioness" (Joel 1:6). "They have the appearance of horses, and like war-horses they charge" (Joel 2:4). Likewise, in Revelation, they "were like horses equipped for battle," and they had lions' teeth. In Joel, their noise was "as with the rumbling of chariots" (2:5). In Revelation, "the noise of their wings was like the noise of many chariots with horses rushing into battle."

But the locust invasion that John sees is immeasurably worse than the one Joel describes. These locusts in Revelation come from "the abyss"—that is, the place destined for the imprisonment of the Devil and his cohorts. Their appearance is impressive, for they at once look like horses armed for battle and like humans with golden crowns—that is, they are both powerful and intelligent—and their tails are like the tails of scorpions, with stingers.

Furthermore, these locusts are organized. The writer of Proverbs 30:27 had marveled that locusts, even without a king, march in rank. These locusts have a king, "the angel of the bottomless pit," whose name is the Hebrew Abbadon and the Greek Apollyon. (Remember the dragon-like figure of Apollyon in John Bunyon's *Pilgrim's Progress*, who is the ruler of this world, the enemy of Christ.) Both of these names mean "destruction." In this, some interpreters see a reference to the Roman emperor, whose title was "king." Since there are reports that Emperor Domitian liked to call himself by the name of the god Apollo, this possibly may be a reference to him and to his divine pretensions, which John has turned into a title of destruction. In any case, the image is one of indescribable suffering—such suffering that people wish to die but cannot.

Picture the congregation in Smyrna, all gathered, listening to this reading, imagining such horrible torments, thinking that there could hardly be anything worse than what they have heard. Then the reader pauses and reads verse 12: "The first woe has passed. There are still two woes to come"!

The Sixth Trumpet
and the Second Woe (9:13–21)

9:13 **Then the sixth angel blew his trumpet, and I heard a voice from the four horns of the golden altar before God,** 14 **saying to the sixth angel who had the trumpet, "Release the four angels who are bound at the great river Euphrates."** 15 **So the four angels were released, who had been held ready for the hour, the day, the month, and the year, to kill a third of humankind.** 16 **The number of the troops of cavalry was two hundred million; I heard their number.** 17 **And this was how I saw the horses in my vision: the riders wore breastplates the color of fire and of sapphire and of sulfur; the heads of the horses were like lions' heads, and fire and smoke and sulfur came out of their mouths.** 18 **By these three plagues a third of humankind was killed, by the fire and smoke and sulfur coming out of their mouths.** 19 **For the power of the horses is in their mouths and in their tails; their tails are like serpents, having heads; and with them they inflict harm.**
20 **The rest of humankind, who were not killed by these plagues, did not**

repent of the works of their hands or give up worshiping demons and idols of gold and silver and bronze and stone and wood, which cannot see or hear or walk. [21] **And they did not repent of their murders or their sorceries or their fornification or their thefts.**

For generations, the most feared enemies of Israel had come from beyond the Euphrates: Babylon and Assyria. Now the same was the case with the Roman Empire, whose most feared enemy was Parthia. Thus, the image of a great invasion from the east was not new for John's readers. The novelty was the magnitude and the consequences of this invasion. The very number of the invaders, two hundred million, was a staggering figure at a time when an army of fifty thousand would have been considered invincible. Even worse, each of these invaders presents a terrifying sight—rather, their horses do, for we are not told that the riders themselves do more than ride.

The horses have lions' heads, and out of their mouths come fire, smoke, and sulfur, which kill a third of the human race. Since we are told that the riders' breastplates were "the color of fire and of sapphire [smoke] and of sulfur," the picture that we apparently are to imagine is that the horses whose riders wore red breathed fire, those whose riders wore sapphire breathed smoke, and those whose riders wore yellow breathed sulfur. Even more terrifying, the horses have tails that are shaped like serpents, with heads of their own, "and with them they inflict harm."

The fact that we are not told that the riders themselves kill anyone and that although the horses' tails "inflict harm" there is no mention of such harm, is an indication that we are to read this description—as the rest of Revelation—as poetic imagery, whose purpose is to convey an impression rather than to describe every detail. Therefore, it would be in vain that we would look for the hidden meaning of the horses' tails, the colors of the riders' breastplates, and so on.

In any case, this great plague would remind readers steeped in the traditions of Israel of the final plague of Egypt, when the angel of the Lord struck down the firstborn of the Egyptians (Ex. 12:29–30) but passed over those households marked with the blood of the passover lamb (Ex. 12:21–23).

This great plague takes place, John tells us, on "the hour, the day, the month, and the year" appointed by God. Again, this would remind his readers that the first Passover took place at the appointed time and that it marked the beginning of the Jewish calendar. Egypt and Pharaoh did not know that their lives and their future were in the hands of God, just as here Rome and the present order do not know that their lives and their future are in the hands of God. Like Pharaoh and Egypt and Rome, all who seek to build their lives and their power apart from God will one day find that theirs is a futile enterprise.

Note that in the case of Egypt, when this final and terrifying plague destroyed the firstborn, Pharaoh finally decided to release the children of Israel. Not so in John's vision. The rebellious who choose to disobey God will remain disobedient even after this final, appalling plague—even after they see one-third of their number destroyed.

This is a lesson that the church has not always heeded. Too often we have thought that we can scare people into believing, or at least into being obedient to God. Some even use the book of Revelation for that purpose. But what Revelation in fact says is that, no matter how dire God's warnings, those who choose not to believe will remain adamant in their disobedience.

THE VISION OF THE LITTLE SCROLL
Revelation 10:1–11

10:1 **And I saw another mighty angel coming down from heaven, wrapped in a cloud, with a rainbow over his head; his face was like the sun, and his legs like pillars of fire. [2] He held a little scroll open in his hand. Setting his right foot on the sea and his left foot on the land, [3] he gave a great shout, like a lion roaring. And when he shouted, the seven thunders sounded. [4] And when the seven thunders had sounded, I was about to write, but I heard a voice from heaven saying, "Seal up what the seven thunders have said, and do not write it down." [5] Then the angel whom I saw standing on the sea and the land**
    raised his right hand to heaven
     [6] and swore by him who lives forever and ever,
who created heaven and what is in it, the earth and what is in it, and the sea and what is in it: "There will be no more delay, [7] but in the days when the seventh angel is to blow his trumpet, the mystery of God will be fulfilled, as he announced to his servants the prophets."

[8] Then the voice that I had heard from heaven spoke to me again, saying, "Go, take the scroll that is open in the hand of the angel who is standing on the sea and on the land." [9] So I went to the angel and told him to give me the little scroll; and he said to me, "Take it, and eat; it will be bitter to your stomach, but sweet as honey in your mouth." [10] So I took the little scroll from the hand of the angel and ate it; it was sweet as honey in my mouth, but when I had eaten it, my stomach was made bitter.

[11] Then they said to me, "You must prophesy again about many peoples and nations and languages and kings."

Once again John brings us to the edge of our seats, only to keep us in suspense. He told us that there were seven angels, each with a trumpet. Presumably, the sounding of the seventh trumpet would bring about the end. But before we get to the seventh trumpet, there are two other passages: the one about the angel with the little scroll and the one about the two witnesses.

This section about the little scroll is patterned after Ezekiel 2:8–3:11, which in some ways is the calling of Ezekiel. Likewise, this section, practically at the exact center of the book of Revelation, validates John's calling as a prophet and indicates that his message, like Ezekiel's, is from on high.

The "mighty angel" coming down from heaven presumably is Gabriel, since his name means "God is my strength." All the images describing him give the impression of power and might: He is "wrapped in a cloud, with a rainbow over his head" (probably indications of his enormous stature); his face is "like the sun," and "his legs like pillars of fire." When he shouts, it is "like a lion roaring," and "the seven thunders [that is, the fullness of thunder] sounded." The message of this great sound, however, is such that John is told to "seal" what the seven thunders have said—that is, to keep it secret—and not write it down. Presumably it is beyond the scope of human words. The entire passage is one of majestic grandeur and dramatic expectation, culminating in the angel's raising his right hand to heaven and swearing that there will be no more delay—presumably in the same loud voice that was like a lion roaring.

But once again John surprises us. After describing this mighty angel with such overwhelming imagery of grandeur and majesty, the focus of the entire passage will center on a "little scroll" (or book) that the angel holds in his hand. This book was already mentioned in the description of the angel (10:2), but in the midst of such grandiose imagery it passed almost unnoticed.

This scroll is different from the scroll with the seven seals that plays such an important role in Revelation 5. First, that was a great scroll, but this is a little one. Second, that scroll was closed with seven seals, but this one is open. Third, the great scroll is handled only by God and by the Lamb, but this scroll passes from the hand of the angel to John. Presumably, this little scroll does not contain all the great mystery of God's eternal purposes, but simply what John is to proclaim to the churches under his charge.

John, like Ezekiel, is told to eat the scroll, and like Ezekiel he comments on its taste—with the difference that Ezekiel says that the scroll was "sweet as honey" (Ezek. 3:3), and John says that "it was sweet as honey in my mouth, but when I had eaten it, my stomach was made bitter" (Rev. 10:10). Presumably, John does not entirely like the message he is to proclaim; but it is God's message, and it is his task to proclaim it.

The text does not tell us what the scroll said or the content of its message. We presume that the message is, in essence, what John is telling the churches by means of his book. John tells us only that he is to "prophesy again about many peoples and nations and languages and kings."

THE TWO WITNESSES
Revelation 11:1–14

11:1 **Then I was given a measuring rod like a staff, and I was told, "Come and measure the temple of God and the altar and those who worship there, [2] but do not measure the court outside the temple; leave that out, for it is given over to the nations, and they will trample over the holy city for forty-two months. [3] And I will grant my two witnesses authority to prophesy for one thousand two hundred sixty days, wearing sackcloth."**

[4] These are the two olive trees and the two lampstands that stand before the Lord of the earth. [5] And if anyone wants to harm them, fire pours from their mouth and consumes their foes; anyone who wants to harm them must be killed in this manner. [6] They have authority to shut the sky, so that no rain may fall during the days of their prophesying, and they have authority over the waters to turn them into blood, and to strike the earth with every kind of plague, as often as they desire.

[7] When they have finished their testimony, the beast that comes up from the bottomless pit will make war on them and conquer them and kill them, [8] and their dead bodies will lie in the street of the great city that is prophetically called Sodom and Egypt, where also their Lord was crucified. [9] For three and a half days members of the peoples and tribes and languages and nations will gaze at their dead bodies and refuse to let them be placed in a tomb; [10] and the inhabitants of the earth will gloat over them and celebrate and exchange presents, because these two prophets had been a torment to the inhabitants of the earth.

[11] But after the three and a half days, the breath of life from God entered them, and they stood on their feet, and those who saw them were terrified. [12] Then they heard a loud voice from heaven saying to them, "Come up here!" And they went up to heaven in a cloud while their enemies watched them. [13] At that moment there was a great earthquake, and a tenth of the city fell; seven thousand people were killed in the earthquake, and the rest were terrified and gave glory to the God of heaven. [14] The second woe has passed. The third woe is coming very soon.

There are few passages in the entire book of Revelation that have proven to be as difficult to interpret as this one. The words are fairly simple, but it is difficult to see to what they may refer. In particular, who are the two witnesses of whom John speaks?

These difficulties have led many interpreters to accept the theory first advanced by German scholar Julius Wellhausen in 1907. Wellhausen believed that John borrowed from an earlier source which spoke of a different time and failed to adapt it entirely to his situation. According to Wellhausen's theory, John's instruction to measure the temple, but not the courtyard outside, is derived from a prophecy uttered by fanatical Zealots who, upon the taking of Jerusalem by Roman forces at the end of the rebellion in the year 70, took refuge in the temple, claiming that God would not allow it to be taken or destroyed. According to the Jewish messianic writings, just before the coming of the Messiah, Moses and Elijah would appear, thus explaining the origin of verse 3. Further proof can be found in a document from the Qumran community—part of the Dead Sea Scrolls—in which the reference to "two olive trees" in Zechariah 4:3 was interpreted as a promise that there would be two messiahs, one a priest and another a king.

At best, this theory is interesting but fails to clarify the meaning of the passage as John wrote it. At worst, it leaves us with the impression that John borrowed a section of his book from other sources but did not take the time to make it relevant to his message and situation.

In truth, we do not have to go that far in order to interpret this passage. We need only remember that in all probability John was a Jewish Christian—as is proven by the abundant traces of Aramaic, the common language of Palestine, in his Greek and by his constant allusions to Hebrew scripture and tradition. He certainly was at odds with those Jews who persecuted Christians—and that may well be what he meant by phrases such as "the synagogue of Satan" (2:9, 3:9). But he was still a Jew, and it was both as a Jew and as a Christian that he opposed the idolatry fostered by the Roman Empire and by the social order in general. He never said, as later other Christians would say, that Israel had been rejected by God. He simply insisted that Christians are also God's people and that the revelation they have received is the true revelation of the God of Israel.

With that in mind, the passage becomes clearer. The measuring of the temple is for the purpose of safeguarding. On this, most interpreters agree. John is told to measure off—today we might say "to cordon of "—"the temple and the altar and those who worship there." What he is measuring off are those who are the true worshipers of God—both Jewish and Christian.

Those who are not true worshipers, no matter how close they might be, are not to be afforded equal protection. The courtyard, the place traditionally reserved for those who were not fully of the house of Israel, is not to be measured. He is told to "leave that out, for it is given over to the nations, and they will trample over the holy city for forty-two months."

Forty-two months are half of seven years. If seven represents fullness, completion, eternity, then half that number would represent the opposite. The power of the nations over the Holy City is transitory. It will pass.

As we read these words, we must remember that Jerusalem had been destroyed by the Romans some twenty-five years earlier. We tend to think of that event only as a tragedy for Judaism. But it was an equal tragedy for Jewish Christians, such as John. Perhaps, as some claimed, the destruction of Jerusalem was in retribution for her sins; still, it was a tragedy that must have rankled every good Jew, Christian or not. From the point of view of the pagans—"the nations"—the destruction of the city was proof that the God of Israel and of Christians was not all that powerful. Now John says that this seeming victory of "the nations" over the faithful will not last forever. Its time is limited, even though "they will trample over the holy city for forty-two months."

At this point "two witnesses" enter the scene. John calls them "two olive trees." In prophetic literature, Israel was often referred to as an olive tree (see for instance Jeremiah 11:16 and Hosea 14:6). It was also a figure of speech that Christians had taken over, for Paul speaks of Israel as an olive tree (Rom. 11:17). The same is true of the lampstand, which had become a symbol of Israel. Thus, what John does here is to speak of two olive trees, of two branches of the people of God: Israel and the church.

These two will prophesy "one thousand two hundred sixty days, wearing sackcloth." One thousand two hundred and sixty days is forty-two months or three-and-a-half years. In other words, the witnesses' time is also limited. They are not to perform this task forever. They wear sackcloth, because this task calls others as well as themselves—the Gentiles as well as Israel and the church—to repentance. They have enormous power, as attested by the prodigies they are able to perform according to verses 5 and 6—prodigies reminiscent of those performed in Egypt at the time of the liberation of Israel. But even their power is for a limited time, until "they have finished their testimony."

At that point "the beast that comes up from the bottomless pit"—a beast we shall meet again in 13:1—makes war on the two witnesses and kills them. They are left unburied in "the great city that is prophetically called Sodom and Egypt, where also their Lord was crucified." This may mean Jerusalem; but most probably it means the entirety of society as presently ordered, which is a society of corruption and oppression and which therefore is worthy of the symbolic names of "Sodom" and "Egypt." In this city, people from all over the world refuse to bury them and celebrate their death, for their preaching had been troublesome to "the inhabitants of the earth."

At this point, John describes the situation of his time: Jerusalem had been destroyed; Jews and Christians had been scattered; their God seemed powerless; and both Israel and the church were like two olive trees that had been cut off—or like two witnesses who had been killed and left unburied, the object of the entire world's mockery.

But this is not the end. The period of the nations' gloating will last only "three and a half days"—again the figure denoting a limited time, but now in terms of days rather than years. The prophets are given renewed life. They are vindicated and drawn up to heaven while their enemies watch them and suffer earthquake and death.

This, says John, is the second woe, and "the third woe is coming very soon."

THE SEVENTH TRUMPET
Revelation 11:15–19

11:15 **Then the seventh angel blew his trumpet, and there were loud voices in heaven, saying,**
> **"The kingdom of the world has become the kingdom of our Lord**
> **and of his Messiah,**
> **and he will reign forever and ever."**
16 **Then the twenty-four elders who sit on their thrones before God fell on their faces and worshiped God,** 17 **singing,**
> **"We give you thanks, Lord God Almighty,**
> **who are and who were,**
> **for you have taken your great power**
> **and begun to reign.**
18 **The nations raged,**
> **but your wrath has come,**
> **and the time for judging the dead,**
> **for rewarding your servants, the prophets**
> **and saints and all who fear your name,**
> **both small and great,**
> **and for destroying those who destroy the earth."**

¹⁹ **Then God's temple in heaven was opened, and the ark of his covenant was seen within his temple; and there were flashes of lightning, rumblings, peals of thunder, an earthquake, and heavy hail.**

Finally, after much expectation, those gathered at the church in Sardis would be listening intently at the events following the blast of the seventh trumpet. To heighten their expectation, just before the blowing of the trumpet the words had resounded: "The second woe has passed. The third woe is coming very soon" (11:14).

But after so much anticipation, what follows the seventh trumpet is rather mild. No fire and brimstone. No fire consuming the heavens and the earth. No plagues of stinging locusts. Instead, we are given a glorious view of worship in heaven.

This has puzzled students of the Bible and has given rise to two interpretations. The first is that the seventh trumpet, being God's final triumph, does not bring with it any particular sufferings or trials, but only the glorious words of worship in heaven in celebration of God's victory. According to this interpretation, a major section of the book ends with chapter 11, and in chapter 12 John begins with a new series of visions that are different and independent from what he has been saying up to now. What then of 11:14, which announces a "third woe"? This, say these interpreters, is probably an addition on the part of a reader who wished John to be consistent and to follow up on the three woes mentioned in 8:13, 9:12, and 11:14.

The second interpretation, which we find preferable, is that the events following the blowing of the seventh trumpet are discussed in the rest of Revelation. The trials mentioned there—especially the bowls of wrath—are the third woe. But before leading his readers into these awesome vistas of pain and struggle, John wishes to reassure them once again that the victory belongs to God. Therefore, here at the end of chapter 11 he offers the majestic view of the heavenly celebration of that victory. While all the struggles described in the chapters to come are taking place on earth, heaven already knows who the victor will be—and so should Christians!

The heavenly liturgy that is described here is similar to what we have seen already. The major difference is that now the "loud voices" and the "twenty-four elders" praise God for the victory that has taken place (vv. 17–18). Also, chapter 11 ends with the opening of "God's temple in heaven," which allows for the ark of the covenant to be seen. According to a Jewish tradition that was fairly common at this time, the temple in Jerusalem, as well as the ark of the covenant, had their prototypes in heaven. The temple in Jerusalem had been destroyed. The ark of the covenant had been lost—or hidden in a cave by the prophet Jeremiah, as one legend held. But in heaven still stood the true temple and the true ark. Now the temple is open, and the archetypal ark may be seen. This is an unparalleled event, accompanied by "flashes of lightning, rumblings, peals of thunder, an earthquake, and heavy hail."

One could say that this passage, at the very center of Revelation, is the high point of the book. Here its message is expressed in a few concise but powerful words: In spite of the raging of the nations, God's power is God's alone, and the time has come "for judging the dead, for rewarding your servants, the prophets and saints and all who fear your name, both small and great, and for destroying those who destroy the earth." Grounded on this message, John's readers in the seven churches of Asia—as well as all his readers throughout the ages, no matter how difficult their circumstances—can face all forms of tribulation, knowing that the victory belongs to the One in whom we have believed.

6. The Cosmic Battle Begins
Revelation 12:1–18

Chapter 12 marks a significant turning point in John's writing. The earlier visions seem to have been almost private, for John's eyes only, that he was to report to the churches. Now there are signs and portents in the sky, cosmic in scope. He is the witness, but the intimacy of private showings is gone. Perhaps the next several chapters are the content of the third woe, promised back in Revelation 11:14. But they represent a new stage in the drama.

The characters change as well. The symbolism of the next several chapters includes two women: one representing the people of God; the other representing the kingdom of this world. Now a dragon or serpent, along with other great monsters, take center stage, all representing the power of evil. The conflict between good and evil is shown in cosmic scale, to end only with the end of the entire old creation. In this sense, chapters 12 through 20 form a unity that has a very different character than the earlier sections of the book.

THE PORTENTS APPEAR
Revelation 12:1–6

> 12:1 **A great portent appeared in heaven: a woman clothed with the sun, with the moon under her feet, and on her head a crown of twelve stars.** [2] **She was pregnant and was crying out in birthpangs, in the agony of giving birth.** [3] **Then another portent appeared in heaven: a great red dragon with seven heads and ten horns, and seven diadems on his heads.** [4] **His tail swept down a third of the stars of heaven and threw them to the earth. Then the dragon stood before the woman who was about to bear a child, so that he might devour her child as soon as it was born.** [5] **And she gave birth to a son, a male child, who is to rule all the nations with a rod of iron. But her child was snatched away and taken to God and to his throne;** [6] **and the woman**

fled into the wilderness, where she has a place prepared by God, so that there she can be nourished for one thousand two hundred sixty days.

Who is this woman? From the rest of the account, a case could be made for several different possibilities. She could symbolize Israel, persecuted so often and almost totally destroyed, yet destined to give birth to the Messiah. She could symbolize Mary, the mother of Jesus. She could symbolize the church, since later in verse 17 it is clear that she has other offspring who will be persecuted. Most likely, the symbolism is multiple and complex. She is the people of God, which includes Israel and Mary and the church. Mary is the biological link between Israel and the church, indicating that God redeemed the people and did not start over with a new people, abandoning the former ones. The twelve apostles also represent such a link with the covenant people, and the twelve stars in her crown point to such a connection. The concluding chapters of Revelation will also stress the role of the twelve as a connecting point between the old and the new (21:12–14).

The woman is clothed with the sun, bright and shining. She is a heavenly being. Yet at the moment she is introduced, she is in the pain of childbirth. In order to understand what these verses meant to their original audience, steeped in the Hebrew scriptures, we need to recall some of the specifics of Genesis 3: the curses on the serpent, the woman, the man, and the earth, all because of sin. In the case of the woman, she will suffer pain in childbirth. So the cosmic woman, clothed with the sun, is also a woman living under the conditions of sin.

She is faced now by the serpent, also in cosmic size. The serpent or dragon has seven heads, ten horns, and all the heads are crowned. This imagery is reminiscent of the seventh chapter of Daniel, in which Daniel relates his vision of four great beasts coming from the sea, the last one with ten horns. The beasts represent kingdoms whose rule is demonic and terrifying to God's people. Here in John's vision, there is a dragon whose rule is even greater and more demonic. Rome is such an empire in John's time. But in this cosmic scale, the dragon is able to destroy not only earth but a third of the stars. The dragon is in direct opposition to the woman, waiting to devour the child that she is about to bring forth.

Steeped in the imagery of Genesis 3, John's hearers would not be at all surprised by this opposition. The curse on the serpent in Genesis 3:14–15 included the prophecy that the offspring of the woman and the offspring of the serpent would be in conflict. Whereas the descendent of the serpent would strike a heel, the seed of the woman would strike the serpent's head a mortal blow. The church understood this as a messianic prophecy.

The early church often referred to Mary, the mother of Jesus, as the second Eve. Her child would undo the damage done by the first Eve and her progeny. This corresponds to Paul's use of the imagery of the first and second Adam in Romans 5:14. In paintings from the Middle Ages on, Mary is often portrayed as the woman clothed with the sun, with the crown of twelve stars on her head and the moon under her feet. That is a very limiting use of the imagery, however, since more than Mary herself is implied by the portent. At the same time, an overzealous desire to ignore Mary is equally limiting. For the early church, Mary was seen as a symbol both of Eve restored and of the church begun.

We are told that the child the woman bore was male and would "rule all nations with an iron rod." This would be a clear indication of the messianic character of the child, for this quotation from Psalm 2 was also a major messianic prophecy for the early church. The psalm begins with God laughing at the way the nations of the world conspire against God and God's anointed. Then the laughter turns to wrath. In Psalm 2:7 we read that God has said to the anointed one, "You are my son; today I have begotten you." Then the son is told that the nations will be given to him and that he will "break them with a rod of iron." So the child the woman brings forth is the anointed one, the true king of all, the Messiah.

This verse from Psalm 2 was quoted earlier in the letter to the church at Thyatira (Rev. 2:26–27), where Jesus says that he will give the authority to rule over nations with an iron rod to those who conquer and continue to do his works. Here in Revelation 12 it is the seed of the first woman who will contend with the terrible offspring of that first serpent in Eden. We are set for a cosmic battle between God and the forces of evil under whose power all the old creation lies. Even this woman, the one who brings forth the Messiah, suffers the pains of childbirth. She also is part of the old creation still to be redeemed by the one to whom she gives birth.

"But her child was snatched away and taken to God and to his throne." There is a strange combination here of cosmic scope and earthly imagery. The woman is no longer in heaven, but in the midst of the old creation where evil holds sway. Her child is born here, and the danger from the dragon lies here, but her child escapes the danger and is taken to God's throne. If one assumes that Jesus is the messianic figure intended, which John does, then one can place all of his earthly ministry, even his death, in that one word "but." What matters in this dramatic picture is that the dragon did not destroy the child. Death may have been a wound in the heel, but the Messiah is alive, beyond death, and is at the throne of God. In the Apostles' Creed, when the church confesses that Jesus has "ascended to heaven and sits at the right hand of God," it makes clear that the work of the Messiah has been completed on earth.

Meanwhile, the woman is left in this old creation. But she is not left defenseless. God has prepared a place for her in the wilderness, where she shall be nourished.

The overtones of the Exodus are unmistakable. The people of God, after the resurrection and ascension of Jesus, are in the wilderness and are nourished by the new manna, the bread from heaven, the Eucharist—joined in a mysterious way with the one who is at the throne of God. The church in John's day would have recognized itself in these words. Its thinking was dominated not only by the Hebrew scriptures but also by the sacraments of Baptism and Eucharist, themselves built on imagery from Israel's life and history. Jesus had referred to himself as the bread from heaven that, unlike the manna of old, would bring life itself to those who ate it (John 6:31–35; 49–58). John's readers would readily understand the parallel, that just as Israel was nourished by the manna in the wilderness on its way to the promised land, so the church is nourished by the body of Christ, the bread from heaven, as it waits in the wilderness until the time of the final reign of God.

How long would this time in the wilderness last? The strange figure of 1,260 days is given—forty-two months; three-and-a-half years. A finite time, endurable because limited. The church is guaranteed its survival, its protection by God against the dragon. The church itself is guaranteed that, but individual Christians are subject to martyrdom—as we have already seen in earlier parts of this book and as we will see again. Any Christian's thought of preserving *"my* life" for the sake of the preservation of the church is not a sentiment Revelation would condone. The church is preserved by God, not by the actions of any Christians.

In one sense, these portents that indicate the coming of the Messiah and his triumph, now at God's throne, are only the beginning of the final struggle. They are the signal that the victory by the Messiah has been achieved. He is now at God's throne. Nothing can change that. But the dragon is still loose.

THE BATTLE IN HEAVEN
Revelation 12:7–12

> 12:7 **And war broke out in heaven; Michael and his angels fought against the dragon. The dragon and his angels fought back, 8 but they were defeated, and there was no longer any place for them in heaven. 9 The great dragon was thrown down, that ancient serpent, who is called the Devil and Satan, the deceiver of the whole world—he was thrown down to the earth, and his angels were thrown down with him.**
>   10 **Then I heard a loud voice in heaven, proclaiming,**
>   **"Now have come the salvation and the power**
>   **and the kingdom of our God**
>   **and the authority of his Messiah,**
>   **for the accuser of our comrades has been thrown down,**
>   **who accuses them day and night before our God.**
>   11 **But they have conquered him by the blood of the Lamb**
>   **and by the word of their testimony,**
>   **for they did not cling to life even in the face of death,**
>   12 **Rejoice then, you heavens**
>   **and those who dwell in them!**
>   **But woe to the earth and the sea,**
>   **for the devil has come down to you**
>   **with great wrath,**
>   **because he knows that his time is short!"**

The scene shifts and a new character, Michael, is introduced. The dragon is now in heaven along with his angels, fighting the great angel Michael and his angels. This is not to undo the victory won by the Messiah or to say that the defeat of evil depends on Michael rather than on God's Messiah. Precisely because that victory has taken place and the one born of the woman has escaped destruction by the dragon, the time has now come for secondary figures to do the mop-up operations.

Before the victory of the Messiah, the dragon's hold was strong. Now, because a mortal blow has been struck, he and his hosts can be defeated. The battle is short and direct. The dragon and his army have no power now, and Michael and his troops defeat them. But the defeat is only in heaven. The concluding battles still have to be fought on earth, though it is clear who will win.

What a strange idea that the dragon—or the serpent or the devil or Satan, for all these names are used here—should still be in heaven! Who is Satan? Clearly nothing is independent of God. All was created by God, and all of God's creation was good. The traditional view is that Satan is a fallen angel, created good by God but who used the freedom given by God to turn away from God. In that case, one might expect that such a fallen angel had left heaven a long time ago, perhaps even before the creation of this earth and its people. The serpent in Eden shows that the devil was fallen and active.

But when we view the whole of scripture, the answer is not that simple. In Luke 10:18, at the point that the proclamation of the kingdom is begun by the seventy disciples, Jesus says, "I watched Satan fall from heaven like a flash of lightning." In Hebrews 9:23 we are told that the heavenly sanctuary needed to be cleansed by the sacrifice of Christ. The powers of evil had not only corrupted the earth, they had also disrupted heaven. The work of the Messiah was not only to free the earth from sin but also to cleanse heaven itself.

Yet all of this must be said within the context of God's power and providence. Evil is never out of God's control, and the overcoming of evil lies only in God's power. The work of the Messiah is God's work, ending the reign of sin. But until that time came, the power of evil had sway over all of creation, including the creation that is in heaven. The Messiah has come. His work has been accomplished. Heaven has been cleansed.

Who is Michael? In Daniel's visions (Dan. 10:18–21), he is the leader of the heavenly hosts. Their specific task is to protect God's people from the dragon and his angels in heaven. In Jude 9, Michael is called an archangel and is said to have argued with the devil over Moses' body.

A hymn intrudes on the narrative of the woman and the dragon. Perhaps it was a hymn John first heard on this occasion in his vision; perhaps it was a hymn known to him already. It is, however, very appropriate and leads to the heart of the matter. Hymns are a constant feature of John's visions. They point to great celebration in heaven. This hymn celebrates the full victory of the Messiah.

The one who has been thrown down, the devil, is here called "the accuser." He brings to God accusations against the faithful ones. He also tempts the faithful to turn away from God's paths, and this leads to the accusations of unfaithfulness. In the Garden of Eden, the serpent entices Adam and Eve to eat the forbidden fruit. In 1 Chronicles 21:1, Satan entices David to take a census of Israel, evidently to be sure that in human terms he had enough to win a battle, rather than trust in God's power. In the first two chapters of Job, Satan accuses Job of being faithful only because things have gone well for him. God therefore lets Satan afflict Job so that his faithfulness can be seen. Job protests his innocence, but he finally discovers that in the face of the Almighty, to protest our innocence is to utter what we do not understand (Job 42:1–3). In Zechariah's vision

(Zech. 3:1–2), Satan is the accuser of the high priest who intercedes for the people. Instead of listening to Satan's accusations, God rebukes Satan and forgives the guilt of the people. In other words, what saves the people is not their innocence but God's forgiveness. Satan proclaims their guilt. God proclaims their forgiveness.

That is the pattern we see in this hymn. Satan is "the accuser of our comrades . . . who accuses them day and night before our God." The response is not that they are innocent and falsely accused. The response of the hymn is that "they have conquered him by the blood of the Lamb." They have lived by the forgiveness given through Christ. Furthermore, they have given their lives testifying to this forgiveness, not to their own innocence. This is the heart of the gospel itself.

The hymn continues: In 12:12 the division between what has been freed from the power of evil and what has not been freed is made quite clear. Heaven can rejoice, for the powers of evil have ended their sway. Satan has been cast out. But he has been thrown down to the earth, so now is not the time for rejoicing here. The earth and the sea must now contend with the devil and his legions, who are aware of the victory of the Lamb. Satan "knows his time is short" because the decisive victory over him has been won, and therefore he is very angry.

A major item on the agenda of this whole book is to answer the questions clearly on the lips of many Christians in John's day: If Christ has won such a victory, why are our lives in this world getting worse rather than better? Why are persecutions increasing? Why does Rome seem to have more and more power over us?" The answer of this hymn is that the woes upon earth can be expected to get worse, now that the devil has only this area in which to work. At this point, the devil is like a wounded animal, much more dangerous because it is mortally wounded.

THE PRESENT DANGER
Revelation 12:13–18

> 12:13 **So when the dragon saw that he had been thrown down to the earth, he pursued the woman who had given birth to the male child. 14 But the woman was given the two wings of the great eagle, so that she could fly from the serpent into the wilderness, to her place where she is nourished for a time, and times, and half a time. 15 Then from his mouth the serpent poured water like a river after the woman, to sweep her away with the flood. 16 But the earth came to the help of the woman; it opened its mouth and swallowed the river that the dragon had poured from his mouth. 17 Then the dragon**

was angry with the woman, and went off to make war on the rest of her children, those who keep the commandments of God and hold the testimony of Jesus.

¹⁸ **Then the dragon took his stand on the sand of the seashore.**

The mischief caused by this wounded dragon now begins in earnest. At the same time, the narrative of the woman who had given birth continues. Before the section on the war in heaven, she had gone into the wilderness to the place of refuge God had prepared for her. It is not clear whether what we find in verse 14 is a simple repetition or whether these words indicate that the woman had left her place of refuge for a time and has now returned. What is clear is that the earliest church did not face the same persecution from the Roman Empire as was now beginning to be faced by the churches in Asia Minor. God protects the woman, giving her eagle's wings in order to go to the wilderness. Her time in the wilderness is the same as the 1,260 days in 12:6 (or the "forty-two months" of 11:2 and 13:5), though expressed differently. The duration now is given as "a time, and times, and half a time"—that is, three-and-a-half years. The message is the same: The church is preserved by God from the power of the devil; "the gates of Hades will not prevail against it" (Matt. 16:18).

The dragon tries to destroy the woman in the wilderness. A great flood is unleashed from his mouth, like a river. There are parallels both to the Exodus and the Flood. Like the Exodus, the faithful need to be rescued from the danger of water. This is a reversal of the Flood story, for in the time of Noah, God created a flood in order to wash evil from the earth (Gen. 6:11–7:24). In this narrative, it is Satan who tries to wipe the faithful from the earth by means of a flood.

However, the woman is rescued. The source of her rescue is significant: It is the earth that comes to her aid. In Genesis 3, part of the curses resulting from sin is a curse on the ground, which became the enemy of humanity, making it difficult for the man to find food (Gen. 3:17–18). Now, as the powers of evil are being challenged, the earth comes to the aid of the faithful, swallowing up the flood that was intended to harm the woman.

No wonder the dragon was angry! First he and his angels were eliminated from heaven. Then he tried to attack the woman who was the symbol of the faithful on earth, but she was out of his range because even the earth, formerly under the power of evil, refused to cooperate and turned against his demonic intentions.

The concluding verses of the chapter set the stage for the dramatic chapters that are to follow. The wrath of the dragon is turned on those who are more vulnerable: the children of the woman, the faithful who are on the earth, those who keep God's commandments, those who remain faithful in their witness to Jesus. These are next in line. These are the ones to whom the entire book is written, and it clarifies for them why the powers of evil are turned against them. Those powers will be described much more fully in the next chapters.

The chapter concludes in a dramatic fashion: The dragon waits on the seashore. He is not finished. Remember that in the hymn that appeared in 12:12, both the earth and the sea shall see woe, because the dragon has been cast down to them. Now the dragon stands between the sea and the earth, about to make his next move. His target: the faithful on the earth.

7. The Conflict on Earth Begins
Revelation 13:1–14:20

The focus of the conflict has been moved to the time and place familiar to the first readers of John's book. Whereas in chapter 12 the vision was cosmic in scope, these chapters, though dealing with supernatural beasts and great conflicts, still deal with political and religious situations contemporary to the churches to whom this book is addressed. Yet the references to the contemporary are cryptic, partly because of their visionary character and partly because of their sensitive political nature.

THE BEAST FROM THE SEA
Revelation 13:1–10

13:1 **And I saw a beast rising out of the sea; and on its horns were ten diadems, and on its heads were blasphemous names. 2 And the beast that I saw was like a leopard, its feet were like a bear's, and its mouth was like a lion's mouth. And the dragon gave it his power and his throne and great authority. 3 One of its heads seemed to have received a death-blow, but its mortal wound had been healed. In amazement the whole earth followed the beast. 4 They worshiped the dragon, for he had given his authority to the beast, and they worshiped the beast, saying, "Who is like the beast, and who can fight against it?"**

5 The beast was given a mouth uttering haughty and blasphemous words, and it was allowed to exercise authority for forty-two months. 6 It opened its mouth to utter blasphemies against God, blaspheming his name and his dwelling, that is, those who dwell in heaven. 7 Also it was allowed to make war on the saints and to conquer them. It was given authority over every tribe and people and language and nation, 8 and all the inhabitants of the earth will worship it, everyone whose name has not been written from the foundation of the world in the book of life of the Lamb that was slaughtered.

9 Let anyone who has an ear listen;
10 If you are to be taken captive,

> into captivity you go;
> **if you kill with the sword,**
> **with the sword you must be killed.**
> **Here is a call for the endurance and faith of the saints.**

A beast emerges from the sea. Perhaps the dragon, standing on the shore (12:18), summoned it forth. Perhaps it arose spontaneously. It is clear, however, that the dragon has control over this beast, so the dragon may very well be understood to have called it from the sea in order to do the dragon's bidding.

The description of the beast is significant in that it bears resemblance to the dragon. (On the basis of some ancient manuscripts, the Revised Standard and other versions add the following to their description of the beast: "ten horns and seven heads.") The body of the beast combines the characteristics of all the beasts in Daniel's vision (Dan. 7:3–7). The sea beast then acts as a proxy for the dragon. The beast represents the Roman Empire, even as the beasts in Daniel's vision represented the political power that sought to destroy God's people then. Remember that from the point of view of Asia Minor the Romans came over the sea, from the West. John puts together the existing imagery from Daniel with the realities of the Roman Empire of his own day.

It is the dragon that gives the sea beast power and authority. It is not that political structures are by nature demonic, but rather that the political structure of the Roman Empire has been taken over by a demonic force. This was not always the case. Paul was quite positive about the Empire, both when he told Christians to honor the public authorities (Rom. 13:6–7) and when he proudly claimed his Roman citizenship (Acts 16:37; 22:25–29). By the end of the first century, however, there had been changes in the emperors' understanding of themselves, which cast an ominous shadow over the empire as far as the Christians were concerned.

John paints the sea beast as a parallel to the Lamb, even as the dragon is parallel to God. The Lamb has been given power and authority as God's agent for the creation of a redeemed people; the sea beast is the dragon's— Satan's—agent for the destruction of such people by creating an unredeemed society, and for that purpose has been given power and authority by the dragon. The Lamb is one who died but has risen. The beast has received a mortal blow, which has been healed. The heavenly gathering worships God and the Lamb; the earthly kingdom worships the dragon and the beast.

The sea beast speaks blasphemous words and has blasphemous names on its heads. Here we come to the crux of the matter for John. Throughout the first century, the Roman emperors had begun to use divine titles for themselves. Earlier, emperors had been considered divine after they died, but now that pattern was changing. There were reports that Domitian, the emperor from A.D. 81–96, wished to be called "lord" and "god." It is not so much that the emperors spoke against the God of the Christians, but rather that, by taking to themselves the titles that belong only to the true God, they set themselves up blasphemously in the place of God. When such blasphemy occurs, the political structures become demonic. This is what happened to the Roman Empire. At the time of John's writing, everyone was not required to worship the emperor, but the handwriting was on the wall. Such a time would come.

In 13:5 the beast is "allowed to exercise authority for forty-two months." The one who permits this is God, whose authority is far greater than the dragon's. God permits the demonic powers to be loose and to attack even the faithful. But the time for this is limited: forty-two months, the symbolic length of time mentioned several times before.

Let us review what various processes or forces are operating during this "time, times, and half a time" or "one thousand two hundred sixty days" or "forty-two months." First, the nations are allowed to trample over the Holy City (11:2); second, the two witnesses prophesy in the Holy City (11:3); third, the woman clothed with the sun is given refuge in the wilderness and protected from the dragon (12:6, 14); and fourth, the sea beast is allowed to utter blasphemies (13:5). This was the length of time that the temple in Jerusalem had been desecrated during the reign of Antiochus Epiphanes, the context for the visions of Daniel. The problem at that time was the same: The political structures had taken on the character of an imperial cult, appropriating for themselves the honor due to God alone. That time ended with the reconsecration of the temple. Here, as mentioned earlier (see the discussion on 11:1–14), it represents a finite time during which the powers of evil are permitted to have power unchecked by God. But it is God who gives this permission, both to test the faithful and to demonstrate the sin of the unfaithful.

The sea beast is allowed to make war on the faithful, even to kill them. The beast also is "given authority over every tribe and people and language and nation" (13:7), even as the Lamb has gathered a people out of "every tribe and language and people and nation" (5:9). The whole population of the earth will be divided into two groups: those who worship the Lamb and those who worship the beast. Faithfulness in this situation means resisting the beast, even when that means death.

John closes this section with a brief poem: "If you are to be taken captive, into captivity you go; if you kill with the sword, with the sword you must be killed" (13:10). The second half has echoes of Jesus' words at his betrayal: "All who take the sword will perish by the sword" (Matt. 26:52). In the setting in Revelation 13 this would seem to be a word to those who persecute the church.

But the whole has echoes of Jeremiah's words, and this seems a more likely parallel in John's setting. Jeremiah twice says: "those destined for the sword, to the sword . . . and those destined for captivity, to captivity" (Jer. 15:2). First these words are part of a prophecy before the Exile, showing the destruction that was to come to faithless Jerusalem. The second time they are words to the Judeans who took refuge in Egypt against God's directions, prophesying the destruction that Babylon would bring to Egypt and therefore to the exiles who had tried to escape it (Jer. 43:11). In Revelation 13:8–10 those whose names are in the Lamb's book of life may be called to suffer. If they are destined to captivity or to death, then it will be so. Like the ancient Judeans, this fate will come to them, whether or not they try to evade it. Therefore, they must endure and be faithful.

THE BEAST FROM THE EARTH
Revelation 13:11–18

> 13:11 Then I saw another beast that rose out of the earth; it had two horns like a lamb and it spoke like a dragon. [12] It exercises all the authority of the first beast on its behalf, and it makes the earth and its inhabitants worship the first beast, whose mortal wound had been healed. [13] It performs great signs, even making fire come down from heaven to earth in the sight of all; [14] and by the signs that it is allowed to perform on behalf of the beast, it deceives the inhabitants of earth, telling them to make an image for the beast that had been wounded by the sword and yet lived; [15] and it was allowed to give breath to the image of the beast so that the image of the beast could even speak and cause those who would not worship the image of the beast to be killed. [16] Also it causes all, both small and great, both rich and poor, both free and slave, to be marked on the right hand or the forehead, [17] so that no one can buy or sell who does not have the mark, that is, the name of the beast or the number of its name. [18] This calls for wisdom: let anyone with understanding calculate the number of the beast, for it is the number of a person. Its number is six hundred sixty-six.

Another beast appears, and with it a lower level of delegation is reached. This beast is from the earth, not from the sea (13:11). It too is related to the dragon's power, but only through the sea beast. The new creature has power in the presence of the sea beast and particularly is related to leading human beings to worship the sea beast (13:12). If the sea beast represents the political structures of the Roman Empire that have taken for themselves titles and authority that belong only to God, then this second beast is most likely related to the local religious and political structures that express the imperial cult. This could involve not only the actual priests of that cult but also many of the traditional local institutions of Asia Minor that were readily compatible with the imperial cult and supportive of it. It may be that part of what is meant by this beast coming "from the earth" is its local character, that it represents local institutions and traditions put at the service of the beast from the sea.

This beast is described as looking like a lamb but sounding like a dragon, indicating the parallel between the powers of the true God and the powers of evil. Evidently, proclaiming and publicizing the divine character of the sea beast and urging its worship is the main task of the earth beast. In this, the earth beast is the counterpart of the two witnesses of 11:3. So the levels of derivation are (1) on the side of the true God: God, the Lamb, and the two witnesses; and (2) on the side of the dragon: the dragon, the sea beast, and the earth beast. Each level is a derivation of the higher one and is parallel to the other chain of actions.

Like the two witnesses, this earth beast urges toward worship, and does signs and wonders, specifically with fire. In fact, the earth beast is quite successful. It urges construction of images of the sea beast—evidently the emperor—in order that it can be worshiped. Furthermore, the earth beast manages to have the image speak as though it were alive (13:15). This may mean either that some miraculous power was actually given to the earth beast or, as evidence a few centuries later shows, that methods were devised to make it possible to have a priest speak through a statue without being seen. What is essential here is the content of the image's speech: Those who do not worship the beast are to be killed.

What we know about this period of time, at the end of the first century A.D., is that emperor worship had increased greatly. Domitian had a statue of himself erected in Ephesus that, judging from the ruins, must have been twenty-three feet tall. There were also temples devoted to emperor worship throughout Asia Minor. These were a new phenomenon, and to John represented a clear danger and threat. Though Christians were not sought out for persecution, they stood in great danger if they came to the notice of the state and refused to recant and refused to perform the worship necessary to show their loyalty to the state.

There is a second great danger from the earth beast: It connects the religious and the economic life of the community in a manner that makes it impossible to participate in the economic sector without being involved in emperor worship (13:16–17). This may refer to the image and titles of the emperor on coinage. It may refer to the religious practices connected with the various trade guilds as mentioned earlier (see the Introduction, the section titled "The First Readers"). In any case, the language in these verses makes the signing of the worshipers of the beast parallel to the signing of Christians in their baptism (7:3). So the followers of the beast are marked with a seal as are the followers of the true God.

The issue is, to whom do human beings belong, to whom do they owe their ultimate loyalty: God or the emperor? There was no such decision to be made as long as the emperor—or the state in whatever form—did not demand ultimate loyalty but rather kept to ordering and organizing community life within clear limits. But when the emperor—or the state— began to go outside of those confines, then conflict was bound to erupt with those who gave their ultimate allegiance to God.

The chapter closes with some of the most enigmatic words to be bound in all of scripture: The number of the beast is 666. Whatever this means, it would have been clear to the original audience but is lost to us. There are various ways of creating numbers out of letters, and the author might have been using either a Hebrew or Greek alphabet. The number seems to mean a particular person—perhaps a public official whose duty was concerned with spreading the imperial cult in Asia Minor by public proclamations or by building programs or by both. The name is in code, either because of the danger of mentioning the name or because the code number indicates it is an incomplete, imperfect number—unlike the perfect 777 or the more-than-perfect 888, which is the number to which the name of Jesus corresponds. We cannot determine the significance of the number 666 at this late date. But that is a minor point in contrast to what we do know about the danger of the earth beast and about the parallels that can occur in our own time.

THE CHALLENGER APPEARS
Revelation 14:1–5

14:1 **Then I looked, and there was the Lamb, standing on Mount Zion! And with him were one hundred forty-four thousand who had his name and his Father's name written on their foreheads.** 2 **And I heard a voice from heaven**

**like the sound of many waters and like the sound of loud thunder; the voice
I heard was like the sound of harpists playing on their harps, [3] and they sing
a new song before the throne and before the four living creatures and before the elders. No one could learn that song except the one hundred forty-
four thousand who have been redeemed from the earth. [4] It is these who
have not defiled themselves with women, for they are virgins; these follow
the Lamb wherever he goes. They have been redeemed from humankind as
first fruits for God and the Lamb, [5] and in their mouth no lie was found; they
are blameless.**

If this were a movie, the theme music would change dramatically as Revelation 14 opens. Instead of the climactic, warlike music that might be appropriate for the sea and earth beasts, we now hear a voice that sounds like
harps and many waters and thunder, accompanied by a choir of 144,000.
This would be familiar theme music to the moviegoers, because it would
have occurred earlier, in 5:6–14. Both then and now, in 14:1–3, the choirs
sing at the appearance of the Lamb. The scene that this theme music ac-
companies is also dramatic: The Lamb is standing on Mount Zion. This
parallels the dragon, who took his stand on the shore (12:18) before the
two beasts appeared in chapter 13. Presumably, the dragon is sill there,
watching the beasts.

Now the Lamb appears on Mount Zion, accompanied by the 144,000-
member choir, who sing the new song. The stage is set for the conflict on
earth. On the side of the dragon are his two proxies: the beast from the sea
and the beast from the earth. On the side of the Lamb there is no exact
parallel, for the 144,000 are not proxies in the same way. They are accompanied by the heavenly figures also encountered in earlier chapters of
Revelation: the twenty-four elders and the four living creatures (4:4–5:14;
7:11–13; 11:16). Though the Lamb is on Mount Zion, he is accompanied
by these heavenly figures.

Who are these 144,000? They are human beings, redeemed by the
Lamb, the first fruits of the redemption achieved by the Lamb (14:3, 4),
which would mean the first fruits of the work of the cross and resurrection. These redeemed have completed their earthly lives in faithfulness to
the Lamb and are now with him. Are they the same 144,000 that were
mentioned in 7:4–8? Those are the redeemed from each of the twelve
tribes of Israel, sealed with God's seal. (Twelve is a perfect, complete
number, far superior to the number 666 given to the earth beast.) The
sealed ones in Israel evidently have now been redeemed, having completed their time of trial faithfully. They form a link between the people
of God in Israel and the new people in the church.

The 144,000 are further described as virgins, who have not defiled themselves with women (14:4). It would be strange if this were meant literally, because the early church did not demand celibacy, though it did have a place for the widows who remained unmarried. This verse needs to be seen in the context of the imagery that begins in chapter 12, with the woman clothed with the sun. Her counterpart, the great harlot, will appear in chapter 17. The bride of the Lamb, who is related to the woman clothed with the sun, appears in chapter 19. The faithful are part of the bride of Christ. They are to keep themselves chaste, not involved with other suitors. Such imagery is used in Ephesians 5 as well as in the Hebrew scriptures where Israel is often pictured as God's betrothed or as the unfaithful wife of God. The 144,000 are the faithful who have remained part of the chaste, virgin bride of Christ. To be unchaste is to commit idolatry, to honor other gods—in this case, the dragon and his associates.

Not only are they chaste, the 144,000 are also truthful. Their witness has been honest and true (14:5). Their words and their deeds have matched. They are martyrs in this sense of being accurate witnesses to the work of the Lamb. They may also have been martyrs in terms of their lives. In this sense also, they have followed the Lamb, even to death.

THE ANNOUNCEMENT OF JUDGMENT
Revelation 14:6–13

14:6 Then I saw another angel flying in midheaven, with an eternal gospel to proclaim to those who live on the earth—to every nation and tribe and language and people. 7 He said in a loud voice, "Fear God and give him glory, for the hour of his judgment has come; and worship him who made heaven and earth, the sea and the springs of water."

8 Then another angel, a second, followed, saying, "Fallen, fallen is Babylon the great! She has made all nations drink of the wine of the wrath of her fornication."

9 Then another angel, a third, followed them, crying with a loud voice, "Those who worship the beast and its image, and receive a mark on their foreheads or on their hands, 10 they will also drink the wine of God's wrath, poured unmixed into the cup of his anger, and they will be tormented with fire and sulfur in the presence of the holy angels and in the presence of the Lamb. 11 And the smoke of their torment goes up forever and ever. There is no rest day or night for those who worship the beast and its image and for anyone who receives the mark of its name."

^{12} **Here is a call for the endurance of the saints, those who keep the commandments of God and hold fast to the faith of Jesus.**

^{13} **And I heard a voice from heaven saying, "Write this: Blessed are the dead who from now on die in the Lord." "Yes," says the Spirit, "they will rest from their labors, for their deeds follow them."**

The scene continues: the dragon on the shore; the sea beast and the earth beast present; the Lamb on Mount Zion; and now three angels appear, one after the other, each with an announcement related to the final judgment of the earth.

The first angel appears in midheaven—that is, in a place visible to all of the earth—proclaiming "an eternal gospel." The content of the gospel is that all should worship the one true God, the Creator of all things. This is in clear contrast to the message of the Empire, that all are to worship the emperor. Judgment is about to begin, and the criterion for judgment is whether or not the individual worships the true God. It is God who is to be feared, to be held in awe. The great temptation is to fear the emperor, or the power of the Empire, more than God.

It is also important to note that God desires the gospel to be proclaimed even up to the point of final judgment. The church should not withdraw from mission and evangelism, and let the evil world go its way. But mission is not only a human effort; it is also a task given to an angel, to make sure that all the inhabitants of the earth are presented with the truth.

The term "gospel" is usually understood by Christians to be the message of redemption through the work of Christ, particularly the work of the cross and resurrection. Here, an eternal gospel is proclaimed that makes no mention of this. But since this gospel is being proclaimed in the presence of the Lamb on his throne, its context includes those elements. At the same time, the redemption through Christ is to lead all people to do exactly what this eternal gospel proclaims: to "fear God and give him glory."

A second angel appears, with the message of the fall of Babylon. For the first time in this book, the term "Babylon" is used, in reference to Rome. John is not the first to use this term in that sense. Other apocalyptic literature of the period also refers to Rome as Babylon. There is good reason for this. In Daniel, the oppressive power was Babylon, and faithful Jews struggled with this empire, which sought for itself the worship due only to God (see Dan. 4:26–37). We have already seen the many images John uses from Daniel. The image of Babylon is the next. Both Rome and Babylon are cities, yet the name is used also for the empire that is ruled from the city. If the city falls, the empire falls. The first Babylonian Empire was the great enemy of

Israel in the eighth century B.C. It conquered and destroyed the Northern Kingdom of Israel centered in Samaria, but the Southern Kingdom of Judah, with its capital in Jerusalem, was left standing. In the sixth century B.C., a new Babylonian Empire captured Jerusalem and destroyed the kingdom of Judah, taking many of its people into exile. Therefore, the term "Babylon" was used to refer to any great power that was the enemy of the people of God.

John personifies the city as a woman—a sinful woman who tempts others to commit fornication with her. Those who do so are obviously not heeding the words of the eternal gospel. The words of the angel who announces judgment are very similar to the words of Isaiah 21:9: "Fallen, fallen is Babylon; and all the images of her gods lie shattered on the ground." Isaiah was speaking of the ancient Babylonian Empire that was about to conquer Jerusalem and Judah in the sixth century B.C.

A second image is added: the cup of wine that is the wrath of God (14:8–10). John pictures the woman Babylon forcing others to drink of this cup. Yet the cup is God's wrath against those who commit fornication with her. Daniel used a variant of this imagery. In Daniel 5, the prophet was called to King Balshazzar's feast in order to interpret the handwriting on the wall. The handwriting began to appear while the king and his court drank wine from the cups brought as part of the booty from the temple in Jerusalem. They drank in praise of the false gods of Babylon. The words on the wall told of the fall of the king and his kingdom. The cup turned into the cup of God's wrath. Jeremiah 25:15–29 also used the imagery of the cup of God's wrath, but it was given to the prophet, who was to give it to various nations to drink. The closest parallel, however, is in Jeremiah 51:7: "Babylon was a golden cup in the LORD's hand, making all the earth drunken; the nations drank of her wine, and so the nations went mad."

For John, the meaning is similar: Babylon—in John's book, Rome—has a cup of wine, and all the people, even other nations, drink from the cup. But the cup is God's wrath, and those who drink from it receive God's wrath. For John, the imagery is made more complex by the personification of Babylon/Rome as a woman with whom the others commit fornication because they worship her rather than the true God. Though the nations drink from the woman's cup, it is really God's cup from which they drink. Babylon is the unwitting agent of God in this matter. The imagery of the cup of God's wrath may lie behind the words of Jesus in the Garden Gethsemane: "If it is possible, let this cup pass from me" (Matt. 26:39). For Christians, part of the mystery of the cross is that Jesus suffered for us the wrath of God that was our due.

A third angel appears. The sequence is important. The first angel proclaimed the gospel and announced judgment. The second announced the fall of Rome. The third announces that all who worship the beast will be condemned (14:9). In fact, those who once drank the wine of Babylon now must drink the cup of God's wrath directly, and it will be an even more powerful wine, unmixed with water. This announcement gives a very clear choice: Worship the beast or the Lamb—but the defeat of the beast has begun and is sure. The worship of the beast is to be seen in the mark that its worshipers bear, even as the worshipers of the Lamb are marked.

It would be possible to understand the messages of these three angels simply as a judgment of those who have been worshiping the beast. More likely, the messages could be a call to those presently worshiping the beast to change their allegiance to the Lamb. The announcement of the gospel is a final point of decision, a final call for those worshiping the beast to see the futility of remaining loyal to one whose doom is sure. The future of those who continue to worship the beast is spelled out: They will drink directly from the cup of God's wrath and burn eternally (14:10). This is seen as part of the warning, giving more reason to make the choice for the Lamb. The vision adds that the suffering of those who worship the beast will occur in the presence of the Lamb and his angels. It is difficult to imagine anyone, most particularly Jesus, enjoying the suffering of others. As part of the warning, however, we clearly are told that the Lamb will completely defeat the beast, and therefore the beast's worshipers need to reconsider the object of their devotion.

The final part of the message of the third angel is important: "There is no rest day or night for those who worship the beast" (14:11). No rest means no sabbath, no time of renewal, no imitation on a human level of the divine life. This is in contrast to the future life of the faithful, shown in the concluding two verses of this section.

The messages of the three angels are over. John adds his own comment of encouragement to those who worship the Lamb: They should continue in obedience. A voice from heaven adds a further promise: Even if the faithful die, they will rest. The Spirit affirms this promise. The deeds of the faithful are not lost, but follow them in the life to come, which evidently is why they can rest. Their time of labor is over. The worshipers of the beast, however, do not have good deeds that can follow them, and therefore they have no rest. It is not that the faithful are saved by their works, but faithfulness does show itself in action, even as the 144,000 were said not to lie, because their lives and their words were consistent (14:5).

THE HARVEST
Revelation 14:14–20

> 14:14 **Then I looked, and there was a white cloud, and seated on the cloud was one like the Son of Man, with a golden crown on his head, and a sharp sickle in his hand!** [15] **Another angel came out of the temple, calling with a loud voice to the one who sat on the cloud, "Use your sickle and reap, for the hour to reap has come, because the harvest of the earth is fully ripe."** [16] **So the one who sat on the cloud swung his sickle over the earth, and the earth was reaped.**
>
> [17] **Then another angel came out of the temple in heaven, and he too had a sharp sickle.** [18] **Then another angel came out from the altar, the angel who has authority over fire, and he called with a loud voice to him who had the sharp sickle, "Use your sharp sickle and gather the clusters of the vine of the earth, for its grapes are ripe."** [19] **So the angel swung his sickle over the earth and gathered the vintage of the earth, and he threw it into the great wine press of the wrath of God.** [20] **And the wine press was trodden outside the city, and blood flowed from the wine press, as high as a horse's bridle, for a distance of about two hundred miles.**

Now the scene changes. Instead of the Lamb, John sees "one like the Son of Man," a term Christians use for Jesus but one also used by Daniel for the one who has authority in the final judgment (Dan. 7:13–14). In Matthew 25:31–46 there is also the famous final judgment scene, with the Son of Man and his angels in charge. Perhaps the most direct parallel to this section of Revelation is in Mark 13:26–27, the "Little Apocalypse" (and its parallel in Matthew 24:30–31). There we are told: "Then they will see 'the Son of Man coming in clouds' with great power and glory. Then he will send out the angels, and gather his elect from the four winds." The picture in Revelation 14:14 is the Son of Man, seated triumphantly on a cloud, wearing the crown of victory. He holds a sickle in his hand. It is time for the harvest.

As we will see in this section, the harvest is of two sorts: of wheat and of grapes. The wheat represents the faithful, those who belong to Christ; the grapes represent those who worship the beast. All of humanity is incorporated in one of these two groups. On other occasions in scripture, there is a division between the wheat and the chaff (Matt. 3:12; Luke 3:17) or between wheat and weeds (Matt. 13:30), but the point is the same. Harvest is the time when the good is separated from the bad.

In Revelation, though the Son of Man has appeared, ready to carry out the judgment, this does not begin until an angel announces that it is time to begin. This angel comes from "the temple," which evidently means directly from the presence of God. In Matthew 24:36, Jesus said that the Son does not know the time of the end; only the Father knows that. The angel declares that the harvest of the earth is ripe; the time has come to gather the wheat. The harvest is gathered from the whole earth by the Son of Man, who uses the sickle himself. The faithful have been gathered, as grain is harvested.

The judgment moves on to the worshipers of the beast. The procedure is different, but parallel. Another angel comes out from the temple, also carrying a sickle, ready for the harvest (14:17). Again, the one with the sickle does nothing until another comes with the message that the time has come. The grapes are now fully ripe, ready for harvest. The second angel who announces the time has come is specified as the angel who has authority over fire—perhaps a sign of judgment, though no fire is mentioned in this section. When the time is announced, the angel with the sickle gathers all the grapes and puts them in the wine press, which represents the wrath of God. It is clear that the Son of Man directly harvests the wheat, but an angel harvests the grapes.

There is a consistency in the imagery in this chapter: The grapes represent God's wrath, both in the wine cup and in the harvest. The winepress as a symbol of God's judgment is used in Isaiah 63:2–6. The final verse in that passage reads: "I trampled down peoples in my anger, I crushed them in my wrath, and I poured out their lifeblood on the earth." These images have been made more familiar by the words of *The Battle Hymn of the Republic:* "He is trampling out the vintage where the grapes of wrath are stored."

In 14:20, the blood from the winepress is said to flow out "as high as a horse's bridle, for a distance of about two hundred miles." There is an added detail here: the winepress is outside of the Holy City. The image is of the Holy City, perhaps with the Son of Man there with the faithful (the grain) gathered nearby. The wicked, those who worshiped the beast, remain outside the city in the judgment carried out by the angel. Outside the city is the area that is unclean; inside the city is the area of purity.

The time of harvest has come, for both the worshipers of the Lamb and the worshipers of the beast. Yet the harvest is not a simple one. The chapters that follow continue the display of the wrath of God upon the earth.

8. The Wrath of God
Revelation 15:1–16:21

THE FINAL WRATH IS ANNOUNCED
Revelation 15:1

15:1 **Then I saw another portent in heaven, great and amazing: seven angels with seven plagues, which are the last, for with them the wrath of God is ended.**

Revelation 15 begins the same way as did chapter 12: a portent appears in heaven. Only three such portents or signs appear in the book of Revelation: the woman clothed with the sun (12:1); the great red dragon (12:3); and now the seven angels who are to dispense the seven plagues (15:1). In the same way that the woman and the dragon ushered in the clear battle between God and Satan, this portent ushers in the final defeat of the powers of evil. They are defeated by the wrath of God, and with their defeat the wrath of God comes to an end. Although verse 15:1 announces the plagues, they do not begin until chapter 16. Why then is chapter 15 included?

There is great drama in this scene, and the description of the giving of the bowls shows the significance of this final expression of the wrath of God. There is actually a word of hope given in this verse, for it is promised that the wrath of God will end. This promise is very important. God's love never ends. God's wrath is a reality, but it is not forever. In Psalm 77:7 the psalmist asks, "Will the Lord spurn forever, and never again be favorable?" But the psalmist is also aware of what Revelation declares: God's warth comes to an end, but God's love does not. It is good that the readers of John's vision are reminded of this truth before they move into the account of the terrible plagues that are to come.

Revelation 15 is brief and divides easily between verses 4 and 5. The first section is the celebration of the blessed ones; the second, is the dramatic description of the giving of the bowls.

THE SONGS OF PRAISE
Revelation 15:2–4

> 15:2 And I saw what appeared to be a sea of glass mixed with fire, and those who had conquered the beast and its image and the number of its name, standing beside the sea of glass with harps of God in their hands. ³ And they sing the song of Moses, the servant of God, and the song of the Lamb:
> "Great and amazing are your deeds, Lord God the Almighty!
> Just and true are your ways, King of the nations!
> ⁴ Lord, who will not fear and glorify your name?
> For you alone are holy. All nations will come and worship before you,
> for your judgments have been revealed."

Those who have conquered the powers of evil personified in the beast with its image and the famous number 666, are gathered to sing. They are around the sea of glass, which 4:6 describes as being in front of the throne. Here it is said that the glass is mixed with fire, perhaps as a sign of the judgment about to occur. These faithful ones have been given harps in order to join in the heavenly chorus, even as there were harps mentioned in the worship scene in 14:2.

We are told that the faithful ones are singing the song of Moses and the song of the Lamb. The parallel of Moses and Christ was very important in the early church. Moses had led the people of God from bondage in Egypt to freedom through the Red Sea. Jesus has led the people of God from bondage—to sin, death, and the powers of evil—to freedom through his death and resurrection. In both cases, a victory has been won.

Exodus 15:1–18 and Deuteronomy 31:30–32:43 both present songs of victory, but the words do not correspond to the one given here. The song of the Lamb may be the new song referred to in 14:3, but no words are given at that point. What is clear is that the songs are songs of victory over enemies. In Exodus 15 the song comes after the crossing of the Red Sea, the escape from Egypt; in Deuteronomy 32 the song occurs shortly before the death of Moses and rehearses God's actions on behalf of Israel from the time of Jacob through the Exodus and beyond. In the brief song given in Revelation 15:3–4 there is no direct statement of victory, but its placement after the announcement of judgment and the final wrath of God upon evil make it a victory song.

In the song, God is the only one to be worshiped, and ultimately all nations will worship God. It is God's holiness that leads to judgment. It is also because of this holiness that all nations should fear the one, true God.

The judgment that is beginning will make that happen. The song is sung before such a victory is made manifest, but those around the throne know that it is guaranteed to occur.

THE BOWLS ARE GIVEN
Revelation 15:5–8

> 15:5 **After this I looked, and the temple of the tent of witness in heaven was opened, 6 and out of the temple came the seven angels with the seven plagues, robed in pure bright linen, with golden sashes across their chests. 7 Then one of the four living creatures gave the seven angels seven golden bowls full of the wrath of God, who lives forever and ever; 8 and the temple was filled with smoke from the glory of God and from his power, and no one could enter the temple until the seven plagues of the seven angels were ended.**

Imagine the scene. There is the temple that contains the throne of God. In front of this is the glassy sea, radiant with fire. Around the sea is the choir of the redeemed, harps in hand. From earlier descriptions we know that the four living creatures and the twenty-four elders on their thrones are here as well (4:4–8; 14:1–3). In Revelation 14, the 144,000 were added to the chorus. This is the setting.

The appearance of the seven angels is dramatic. After the song is sung, the doors of the heavenly temple open, and the seven angels come out. They are described as dressed in priestly garments, with shining white linen robes and golden sashes across their chests. This parallels the dress of "the one like the Son of Man" in 1:13 and the heavenly figure of Daniel 10:5.

One of the living creatures hands out the bowls. The seven bowls parallel the seven seals and the seven trumpets encountered earlier in Revelation 6, 8, and 9. As we have seen, seven implies completion and fulfillment. Here it is the wrath of God, in the form of seven plagues, that is to be completed.

We are not used to hearing much about the wrath of God. It does not seem in keeping for a loving God to be wrathful. But John understands quite well that the holiness of God ultimately requires the destruction of evil. Redemption involves the end of the power of evil. Grace is central, for all human beings are sinful and need forgiveness. But forgiveness alone does not destroy evil. The destruction of evil is the goal of God's wrath. This wrath is for the sake of redemption, for the sake of holiness, not the result of an irrational anger. In the book of Revelation, God's wrath seeks to destroy particularly those sources of evil that are Satan or the instruments of Satan. Human beings must choose to whom their loyalty is given, but the major focus is on the superhuman objects of faithless human worship.

Martin Luther called the wrath of God the work of God's left hand, whereas grace was the work of God's right hand. What he meant was that grace is the ultimate work of God but that wrath was the necessary adjunct to that work. One of the great heresies against which the church had to battle in the second century—shortly after John's book was written—was the thought that the God of Jesus Christ was a God of love and grace, in whom there was no judgment or wrath. The church declared very clearly that this was not true. The same God who redeems is the God who judges and condemns. Without such condemnation of evil, even grace loses its character.

For that reason, the understanding of the cross of Christ includes the fact that Jesus suffered the wrath of God for us, taking on himself God's righteous desire to destroy evil. Therefore, the recipients of grace are to become holy. Grace is not a way for us to indulge in evil without any consequences. Rather, grace is the means by which God frees sinful people from the power of evil so that they may become holy. To eliminate wrath from God is to cheapen and make meaningless the work of grace. This portion of Revelation not only speaks of the wrath of God as a reality but, as we have seen, also points to the end of such wrath, when all of the forces of evil have been destroyed.

Once the seven angels receive their bowls of wrath, the temple from which they have come is filled with smoke, the sign of God's presence. From then until the time of wrath is over, no one can enter the temple. Smoke or cloud is the sign of the presence of God, the glory of God (Ex. 19:18; Isa. 4:5). God's presence is in the temple, but no creature is to be there.

What does this strange note mean? Why is the temple, the presence of God, not available to any creature until the judgment is over? Two reasons may be put forth. The first is that final judgment is in God's hands alone. No creature takes part in this. Even the living creatures and the angels are simply agents of God, carrying out God's will. They cannot enter the temple to assist in making the final decisions. Second, this is the *final* judgment. The time for seeking God's mercy is over. Many warnings have been given; many calls to repentance have been issued. Now that time is past. The doors to the temple are closed to all creatures until the judgment is over. Then even more dramatic events will occur. The temple itself will disappear (21:22).

THE FIRST THREE PLAGUES
Revelation 16:1–7

16:1 Then I heard a loud voice from the temple telling the seven angels, "Go and pour out on the earth the seven bowls of the wrath of God."
² So the first angel went and poured his bowl on the earth, and a foul and painful sore came on those who had the mark of the beast and who worshiped its image.
³ The second angel poured his bowl into the sea, and it became like the blood of a corpse, and every living thing in the sea died.
⁴ The third angel poured his bowl into the rivers and the springs of water, and they became blood. ⁵ And I heard the angel of the waters say,
    "You are just, O Holy One, who are and were,
        for you have judged these things;
    ⁶ because they shed the blood of saints and prophets,
        you have given them blood to drink.
    It is what they deserve!"
⁷ And I heard the altar respond,
    "Yes, O Lord God, the Almighty,
        your judgments are true and just!"

In the same way that the Son of Man and the angel waited until the command came to reap the harvests of wheat and grapes (14:15, 18), so the seven angels wait until the command comes to begin pouring out the seven bowls of God's wrath (16:1). This detail adds to the drama of the scene. It also makes clear that God is in charge of the action carried out by others.

As soon as we hear about plagues, the parallel with the plagues commanded by Moses against the Egyptians comes to mind. Clearly there are intentional parallels, especially since John has just made reference to the Song of Moses. At the same time, there are other portions of the Hebrew scriptures that provide some of the structure to this section of Revelation. One of the most significant is Leviticus 26:1–33. This passage is set as instructions given by God to Moses in the tabernacle after the covenant is established at Sinai. After twenty-five chapters of laws and procedures in the book of Leviticus, chapter 26 gives a list of rewards for Israel if they are obedient and of punishments if they are disobedient.

When the Hebrew people were in bondage in Egypt, God heard their cry and came to their aid. As long as Egypt refused to let them go, God directed Moses to let loose various plagues upon them. There were ten plagues in all. After each one, the pharaoh refused to let the people go, and another plague was announced, until the tenth: the death of the firstborn.

At that point, the pharaoh repented (Ex. 7:14–12:33). Now, after the Hebrews were safely away from Egypt and the covenant with God had been established, the people of Israel were told that Israel will also be a subject of plagues. In the same way as Egypt was given the possibility of repenting after each plague, so Israel was told that the next plague will not occur if they become obedient. The plagues include disease, invasion, famine, wild animals, and exile.

This is a very important word for the church, both in John's day and in ours. Christians may be tempted to think that because they are God's people, God cares for them, and nothing they do can change that. But God is much more even-handed than that. If God's people begin to act like the oppressive forces from which they have been freed, they can expect the same punishments that their former oppressors received. As we saw in the discussion on Revelation 15:5–10, God's wrath is for the purpose of creating a holy people. If God's own people are unholy, they can expect God's wrath to be turned on them.

In rapid succession, the bowls held by the first three angels are emptied. These plagues are of much greater extent than those let loose by the angels with trumpets who appeared after the seventh seal was opened (8:1–9:21), since that series destroyed one-third of the earth, whereas these plagues leave nothing unaffected.

The first bowl leads to painful sores on all who have the mark of the beast. The sores could be boils, leprosy, or some other malady. If the disease is leprosy, there is an added sense of uncleanness, according to Hebrew law. Whatever the source of the sores, those who had been marked with the sign of the beast, perhaps in a hidden fashion, now bear a mark visible to all. Before judgment, human beings may be dishonest regarding where their ultimate loyalty lies, even to themselves. They may appear to be worshipers of the true God, yet in truth they are disciples of the dragon. In the judgment, however, what has been hidden will be made visible to all.

The second angel's bowl changes the water of the seas into blood. This is worse than the first plague against the Egyptians, because the blood is described as the blood of a corpse. According to Hebrew law, this too would be a greater uncleanness, beyond simply blood. Everything in the seas dies.

The third angel pours his bowl, and the fresh-water rivers and springs also turn to blood. After this, there is an interlude in the narrative in which "the angel of the waters" sings a hymn. Who is this angel? There was a belief at the time of John that each of the elements of the earth had an angel in charge of it. This could mean, then, that the angel in charge of water had no objection to its contamination, because the angel represented God, and it was God's righteous judgment that was being executed by means of the water. Or it could refer to the angel who had poured the bowl, destroying the water. As in the hymn in 15:3–4, there is an emphasis on the holiness of God that necessarily leads to judgment. The hymn in 16:5–6 shows that the changing of water into blood is an appropriate punishment for those who have shed the blood of the saints.

After the hymn is sung, "the altar" responds, approving of what had been sung. In 6:9–10, the souls of those who had been martyred are said to be under the altar, from where they cried out for judgment on their enemies. Here, when that judgment is occurring, the souls of the martyrs add their amen.

Visible uncleanness, sinfulness made manifest—that is the bottom line of the first three plagues. Judgment has to do with bringing to light what has been hidden, as well as punishing and rewarding.

THE FOURTH AND FIFTH PLAGUES
Revelation 16:8–11

> 16:8 The fourth angel poured his bowl on the sun, and it was allowed to scorch them with fire; ⁹ they were scorched by the fierce heat, but they cursed the name of God, who had authority over these plagues, and they did not repent and give him glory.
> ¹⁰ The fifth angel poured his bowl on the throne of the beast, and its kingdom was plunged into darkness; people gnawed their tongues in agony, ¹¹ and cursed the God of heaven because of their pains and sores, and they did not repent of their deeds.

After the hymnic interlude, the next two angels pour their bowls. The pattern is different here, for after each of these two plagues it is stated that those against whom the plagues were unleashed did not repent and give God glory or that they cursed God and did not repent. Even at this late stage of judgment, repentance is possible for those who up to that point have worshiped the beast. There is no statement that God intentionally hardens the hearts of those who worship the beast. Yet, there is no indication that anyone does repent at this late date.

The plague of the fourth angel is an increase in the power of the sun, leading to a scorching of the earth, or at least of the unfaithful on the earth (16:8). Now that all the water, both salt and fresh, has been radically polluted, the heat becomes unbearable.

Although the victims are aware that God is the source of these plagues, and although they know that repentance for their worship of the beast is required, they do not repent. In addition to repentance for their past false worship, they are to give God glory. This they also refuse to do. There is a close correspondence between what the unfaithful refuse to do here and the words of the angel preaching "an eternal gospel" from midheaven (14:7). The proclamation of that gospel is that all people are to give God glory and to acknowledge that God is the creator of all things, including both the sea and the springs of water. Now those elements have become unavailable to the sufferers, and still they refuse to worship or glorify God. Because of their continued lack of repentance, the fifth angel pours the bowl of the next plague.

The fifth plague is of a very different character. Instead of focusing on the followers of the beast, this plague falls directly on the throne of the beast. The angel pours the bowl on the throne—the headquarters of the dragon's earthly rule—and the beast's whole kingdom becomes dark. This has overtones of the ninth plague against the Egyptians, which cast the whole kingdom in darkness (Ex. 10:21). Those who worship the beast are also part of that kingdom. Even this awareness of the power of God over the beast does not dissuade its followers from remaining faithful to the beast. Instead of repenting, they curse God.

The fourth and fifth plagues are almost opposites: one bringing too much sun; the other blotting out all light. Only these two plagues are related to the lack of repentance. Both the increase in the sun's light and the darkness of the beast's headquarters lead to blindness.

Whereas the first three plagues brought to light the inner uncleanness of those who worshiped the beast, these two plagues show the blindness of the followers of evil. With such blindness, there can be no repentance. They are locked into their loyalty to the beast. They can see no other way.

THE SIXTH PLAGUE
Revelation 16:12–16

16:12 **The sixth angel poured his bowl on the great river Euphrates, and its water was dried up in order to prepare the way for the kings from the east.** [13] **And I saw three foul spirits like frogs coming from the mouth of the dragon, from the mouth of the beast, and from the mouth of the false prophet.** [14] **These are demonic spirits, performing signs, who go abroad to the kings of the whole world, to assemble them for battle on the great day of God the Almighty.** [15] **("See, I am coming like a thief! Blessed is the one**

who stays awake and is clothed, not going about naked and exposed to shame.") [16] **And they assembled them at the place that in Hebrew is called Harmagedon.**

The sixth plague is much more complicated. First, it is more geographically specific: The river Euphrates dries up, so that enemies of Rome can come across it in invasion. There was a real fear in Rome that Parthia, on the east, would invade. But this plague also represents a reversal of the Exodus events. Instead of a dry river being a sign of salvation, it is a sign of defeat. The kings from the East are a prelude to the greater gathering of kings from the whole world that will be described in 16:14.

As part of the sixth plague, the unholy trinity—the dragon, the beast from the sea, and the false prophet who is the beast from the earth—appear with evil spirits like frogs coming out of their mouths. The frogs have overtones of the second plague on Egypt (Ex. 8:2–6). John's vision makes many references to speech: false prophecy, faithful witness, telling the truth, true worship, idolatry—all of which come from the mouth. Here, the frogs that are evil spirits come from the mouth, setting the scene for the coming conflict between those who speak falsely and the one who speaks truth (19:11–15).

These evil spirits like frogs perform signs, by means of which they gather together the kings of the earth. The dragon and his subordinates are seen by others to be successful and powerful; because of this, the rulers of earthly kingdoms come to follow the dragon. The dragon convinces them that their future depends on doing battle with the one true God, who is their enemy.

There is a strange interruption in the narrative about the sixth plague: the words of Jesus in 16:15. They bear a resemblance to passages in the Synoptic Gospels about being watchful and prepared for the Second Coming (see Matt. 24:43–44). Paul uses a similar expression to urge Christians to remain ready for the coming of Christ (1 Thess. 5:2). There are also parallels to the message of Jesus to the church at Laodicea (3:18–22).

To whom are these words of Jesus in Revelation directed? They could be an invitation to repentance for the unfaithful. Yet it would appear they are directed to the faithful, urging them to remain watchful and alert as all of these terrible things happen. If so, this is the first reference to the faithful since the plagues began. If the faithful are still on the earth, they must be affected by most of the plagues, especially those altering the waters, the strengthened sun, and the pervading darkness. Whatever the case may be, a clear mental dramatization of this section is difficult.

After this brief word from Jesus, the narrative goes on to indicate that all the kings, summoned by the dragon and his deputies, gather at the place called Harmagedon. They do so because they believe the signs that have been given: the success and apparent power of the demonic spirits. It is their self-interest that brings them there. The place—Harmagedon—may have been clear to Christians in the late first century, but it is not to us. Some scholars believe that "Harmagedon" is a corruption of "Megiddo," where the kings of Canaan had been defeated by the Israelites (Judg. 5:19). It is not possible to specify where Harmagedon is. In any case, John may not have been thinking of a specific geographical site as much as a symbolic place where the enemies of God are finally conquered.

THE SEVENTH PLAGUE
Revelation 16:17–21

16:17 **The seventh angel poured his bowl into the air, and a loud voice came out of the temple, from the throne, saying, "It is done!"** [18] **And there came flashes of lightning, rumblings, peals of thunder, and a violent earthquake, such as had not occurred since people were upon the earth, so violent was that earthquake.** [19] **The great city was split into three parts, and the cities of the nations fell. God remembered great Babylon and gave her the wine-cup of the fury of his wrath.** [20] **And every island fled away, and no mountains were to be found;** [21] **and huge hailstones, each weighing about a hundred pounds, dropped from heaven on people, until they cursed God for the plague of the hail, so fearful was that plague.**

The seventh angel pours out the seventh plague into the air. Even as the angel had proclaimed the eternal gospel in the air—in midheaven—so that all the inhabitants of the earth could hear it (14:6), so the seventh angel pours out the bowl of wrath in the air so its effects will be felt by the whole earth.

At the same time, a voice from the temple cries: "It is done!" This parallels the final words of Jesus from the cross in the Gospel of John: "It is finished" (John 19:30). The words "done" and "finished" are different in Greek, as in English, and have nuances that do not mean quite the same thing. In both cases, however, the work of salvation is completed. In Revelation, it is the work of overcoming evil. In John, it is the earthly redemptive work of Christ, upon which the final overcoming of evil is based. In Revelation, good is clearly—finally—overcoming evil. In the gospel, evil appears to have overcome good until the resurrection, which is known

only to the faithful. "It is done" and "It is finished" are two different levels of the same battle. In both cases, from the human perspective it may
not appear that anything is done at the point that the words are being said.
But since the One who utters the words is the One under those providence
all things exist, the words are the guarantee that all that is necessary has
been accomplished.

What are the results of the seventh bowl of wrath, now poured into the
air? Dramatic events of nature follow: earthquakes, lightning and thunder, and, finally, hailstones. Human beings are accustomed to all of these
events, but the scale is beyond anything those on earth have ever seen.
Verse 19 states that "the great city was split into three parts." There is no
scholarly agreement as to what city is meant in this verse. There are two
candidates: Rome and Jerusalem. Rome is generally considered the more
likely candidate.

"The wine-cup of the fury of his wrath" had already been promised in
14:10 to those who followed the beast. Now it is promised to the city of
Rome itself. The content of that fury is spelled out in the next chapters,
though the disasters of nature that are described here are part of that destruction. Islands and mountains disappear. God's vengeance is coming,
and there will be no impediments to the progress of that vengeance. The
opening of the sixth seal had a parallel terror (6:14). This is similar to
the picture given in Isaiah 40:3–5 of the coming of the Lord, where all the
mountains will be made low and the valleys lifted up. That verse is quoted
by Luke, describing the ministry of John the Baptist (3:5). In Revelation
16:20, it is not for the sake of God's redemption that the path is made
ready, but rather for the swift coming of God's wrath.

The seventh plague ends with the hailstorm, with hailstones weighing
a hundred pounds falling on people. Even this does not change the hearts
of those who worship the beast. When the storm becomes totally unbearable, they curse God, rather than repent and turn to him.

The sequence of the seven bowls of wrath has been completed. That
does not mean the judgment is over. In a sense, it has only begun. The
plagues have brought no repentance. The evil of the beast has been revealed for all to see. Those who follow the beast curse God, rather than
give God glory. What follows is the description of the evil empire and its
followers who have been judged.

The failure of the bowls of wrath to bring about any change of heart is
important. Not only is it not possible to terrify people into faith, those
who follow an evil path often do so because it seems successful. The risk
of giving up the security of the old way is too great. The way of faith seems

extremely insecure and does not lead to the same rewards. The beast and its followers have been powerful and successful. The followers of Christ have been poor and unsuccessful in worldly terms. Why should their way be followed? In that frame of mind, each new call to God's way can be interpreted as a threat to the known path to success. In the next chapter we catch a glimpse of exactly how successful the followers of the beast have been.

9. The Fall of Babylon
Revelation 17:1–18:24

PRIDE GOES BEFORE A FALL
Revelation 17:1–6a

> 17:1 Then one of the seven angels who had the seven bowls came and said to me, "Come, I will show you the judgment of the great whore who is seated on many waters, ² with whom the kings of the earth have committed fornication, and with the wine of whose fornication the inhabitants of the earth have become drunk." ³ So he carried me away in the spirit into a wilderness, and I saw a woman sitting on a scarlet beast that was full of blasphemous names, and it had seven heads and ten horns. ⁴ The woman was clothed in purple and scarlet, and adorned with gold and jewels and pearls, holding in her hand a golden cup full of abominations and the impurities of her fornication; ⁵ and on her forehead was written a name, a mystery: "Babylon the great, mother of whores and of earth's abominations." ⁶ And I saw that the woman was drunk with the blood of the saints and the blood of the witnesses to Jesus.

The continuity of this vision with the preceding one is seen in the identity of the angel as one of the seven who had been part of the destruction (17:1). A new image is given: The city is pictured as "the great whore who is seated on many waters." Although this is the first time the city has been referred to as a whore, the fact of her many fornications was made clear earlier (14:8).

She is said to be seated "on many waters," which reflects the fact that all of the rivers and seas lead to her doorstep, a characteristics of her imperial power.

On the forehead of the woman on the beast is the mysterious name: "Babylon the great, mother of whores and of earth's abominations" (17:5). Those who read this passage would have known that Rome was intended. Rome was viewed as the source of great idolatry and other evils, which is clearly the way Christians would have seen the situation at the time. After all, it was the Roman Empire that required them to be involved in idolatrous behavior or else be considered dangerous or excluded from the majority of the economic and social aspects of the community. "The mother of whores" implies that Rome has subverted other institutions so that they also are idolatrous.

As we shall see, goods from all over the world came to Rome from throughout her sphere of influence. The personification of Rome as a woman is important, not only because the imagery of harlotry as unfaithfulness is significant but also because the image of this woman is the negative counterpart of the woman clothed with the sun (12:1–6) and of the bride, whose appearance will climax the final chapters of the book.

Rome is pictured as a woman who has committed fornication with "the kings of the earth," with the powerful leaders of many nations who have traded with Rome and given gifts to her in return for her favors (17:2). The kings have gained much in this process, and so have many of the people. They have grown accustomed to the gifts of Rome and "have become drunk" with all that has come from Rome. What will happen to these kings of the earth and to the others who have been involved with Rome, now that she is to be destroyed? Their future has become intertwined with Rome's fate.

The angel takes John away to the wilderness "in the spirit" (17:3). "In the spirit" is the sign of the visionary character of the writing. John said that the whole vision occurred while he was "in the spirit on the Lord's day" (1:10). He was "in the spirit" when he saw the vision of the heavenly throne (4:2). Here the vision takes him "in the spirit" to the wilderness. When the bride appears, he will be taken "in the spirit" to a mountain.

These four occurrences signal significant shifts in the ongoing vision. The fact that when he sees the fate of "the great whore" he is taken to the wilderness is important. In Chapter 12, verses 5 and 14, the red dragon (Satan) pursued the woman who gave birth to the son into the wilderness. But she has also been protected by God in the wilderness.

Now John sees the great whore seated on a red beast in the wilderness. This is the beast from the sea in 13:1, with ten horns and seven heads and blasphemous names on its heads (17:3). Not only is the beast red, but the whore is dressed in scarlet and purple, complete with gold and jewels (17:4). She is rich and powerful but is carried on the beast, which is the agent of Satan. Those who deal with her are therefore also dealing with Satan. The blasphemous names are titles that should only be applied to God but have been applied to the Emperor.

Robed in luxurious garments, rich with jewels and gold, holding a golden cup filled with impurities (perhaps the cup she has given to "the kings of the earth" [17:2]; perhaps the same cup mentioned in 14:8), Babylon (Rome) rides on the beast, apparently secure, in charge of her own destiny and the destiny of those who have allied themselves with her. Yet all is not well. The kings of the earth have become drunk. They are not clearly aware of what is going on. The great whore is also drunk, but she is drunk with blood—the blood of those who have died faithful to Jesus, his true witnesses. As is typical of visions, the images merge and blur: The cup is the blood of the saints but is also the cup of God's wrath, coming because of Rome's idolatry and persecution. The beast that does the dragon's bidding now carries the great whore who seduces other nations.

WHO IS SHE?
Revelation 17:6b–14

17:6b **When I saw her, I was greatly amazed. ⁷ But the angel said to me, "Why are you so amazed? I will tell you the mystery of the woman, and of the beast with seven heads and ten horns that carries her. ⁸ The beast that you saw was, and is not, and is about to ascend from the bottomless pit and go to destruction. And the inhabitants of the earth, whose names have not been written in the book of life from the foundation of the world, will be amazed when they see the beast, because it was and is not and is to come.**

⁹ **"This calls for a mind that has wisdom: the seven heads are seven mountains on which the woman is seated; also, they are seven kings, ¹⁰ of whom five have fallen, one is living, and the other has not yet come; and when he comes, he must remain only a little while. ¹¹ As for the beast that was and is not, it is an eighth but it belongs to the seven, and it goes to destruction. ¹² And the ten horns that you saw are ten kings who have not yet received a kingdom, but they are to receive authority as kings for one hour, together with the beast. ¹³ These are united in yielding their power and authority to the beast; ¹⁴ they will make war on the Lamb, and the Lamb will conquer them, for he is Lord of lords and King of kings, and those with him are called and chosen and faithful."**

John is amazed at what he sees, so the angel gives him an explanation, which is clearly also for the benefit of John's readers. As an explanation it is strange, for it leaves present readers with even more questions than they had before the explanation was given. Perhaps readers of the first century understood the references more readily, but they are not obvious to us.

The main issue is the identity of the beast—or, more specifically, the significance of the seven heads and ten horns.

Several elements of thought current at the time need to be understood. The imagery of Daniel was known within the Christian community. In Daniel 7:7–28 the description of the fourth beast included ten horns, and the explanation given was that the ten horns were ten kings, and another horn appears, speaking arrogantly.

Much of this parallels the blasphemous speech of the beast in Revelation 17. The vision of John may well have taken over the description of the beast, without trying to represent specific kings. The ten kings evidently represent nations that follow Rome. Some Romans believed that Nero, the Roman emperor who was responsible for persecution of Christians in Rome and who died in A.D. 68, would return to life and lead the empire again.

The seven heads have two explanations. First, they are the seven mountains upon which the woman is seated. That is a surprise, because she was seated on the beast earlier in the vision. Rome's seven hills are the most likely meaning. But then we are told that the seven heads also represent seven kings; evidently Roman emperors are intended. An eighth appears after the seven, in what may well refer to the expectation of Nero's return. There have been many interpretations trying to apply the seven/eight heads to the emperors of the period. If Nero is meant, there would be an interesting parallel between the Christian expectation of the return of Jesus, ushering in the kingdom, and the secular expectation of the return of Nero, ushering in a renewed empire.

In 17:8 it is said that the beast "was and is not and is to come." This is a negative form of the words describing the Lord God in 1:8: " 'I am the Alpha and the Omega,' says the Lord God, who is and who was and who is to come, the Almighty.' " The eternity and omnipotence of God are contrasted with the emperor who, even if he were to come to life again, would be limited in both time and power.

The origin of the beast is clear—it arises from the bottomless pit, the opposite of heaven. The beast will be destroyed after a brief time on earth. Everyone will be amazed when the beast that "was and is not" returns to life—everyone but those who are faithful: the saints whose names are written in the book of life. Two different futures, two different salvations are anticipated: one based on an emperor such as Nero and one based on Jesus Christ—a renewed Roman Empire or the city of God. Many of the rulers of the earth had made their decision, serving the Roman Empire.

Christians have placed their faith in Christ and the future that he will bring. The ten kings represent those nations and rulers who have made their decision in favor of Rome. In 17:13 it is said that they "are united in yielding their power and authority to the beast." They are allies of Rome. Their common enemy is the Lamb, against whom they will wage war. Thus Christians should expect to be persecuted. Their persecution is a sign of the alliance Rome has made with other kings, so that there is no clear hiding place, no safe haven where Christians will not be subject to persecution.

But the outcome of the war against the Lamb is already decided: Rome and her allies will be defeated rapidly. It is the Lamb who is Lord of lords and King of kings, not the Roman emperor who fancies such titles for himself. The Christians who remain steadfast, who do not join in the support of Babylon (Rome) and the ten kings, show themselves to be called, chosen, and faithful. They are called by Christ, chosen by God, and they have shown themselves faithful.

HER FRIENDS BECOME HER ENEMIES
Revelation 17:15–18

> 17:15 **And he said to me, "The waters that you saw, where the whore is seated, are peoples and multitudes and nations and languages. [16] And the ten horns that you saw, they and the beast will hate the whore; they will make her desolate and naked; they will devour her flesh and burn her up with fire. [17] For God has put it into their hearts to carry out his purpose by agreeing to give their kingdom to the beast, until the words of God will be fulfilled. [18] The woman you saw is the great city that rules over the kings of the earth."**

The angel continues with the explanation of the vision. Rome is clearly an empire. Subject to it directly and part of its sphere of influence are non-Romans: Egyptians, Syrians, Greeks, Britons, North Africans, as well as nations not conquered but economically tied by trade. Goods from all over the world pour into Rome. These are the "peoples, multitudes, nations, and languages." They are allies of Rome. But the vision takes a dramatic turn: Precisely these people, Rome's own allies, will turn against her and be the means of Rome's destruction. Her friends will become her enemies, and God's judgment upon her will be carried out by these kings, who once were part of her attack force against the Lamb. This does not mean that the ten kings of the earth have been transformed into followers of God. Rather, they are used by God as instruments of God's judgment against Rome, even when they do not know God. By their support, they have set Rome up for a great fall. They will also be agents of that fall.

Those who allied themselves with Rome did so because it was to their advantage. Their friendship was dependent on what it brought them. If their interests had been served better by turning on Rome, by taking what she had accumulated, then there would have been no reason for them to remain loyal.

In John's day, the *pax romana* was strong. Peace in the area was kept by the strength of Rome. Uprisings were easily stopped. Order was kept by military power. This same power gave Rome the economic advantage over her neighbors. But if any weakness in the empire became apparent, those who had been held in check by Rome's power could readily turn on her and become her enemies. The ten kings are allied with Rome for their own gain. Their friendship is not at all secure if circumstances should change.

John's vision predicts that the time will come when Rome's "friends" will become the agents of her destruction. Even the beast will cease to use Rome for its purposes and will use the other nations as destroyers of Rome. God's judgment on Rome will be carried out by those who have no intention of serving God's purposes or of even acknowledging the one true God. God remains their creator and ruler, and their evil can be turned to God's purposes.

THE FALL OF BABYLON
Revelation 18:1–3

> 18:1 **After this I saw another angel coming down from heaven, having great authority; and the earth was made bright with his splendor.** 2 **He called out with a mighty voice,**
> **"Fallen, fallen is Babylon the great!**
> **It has become a dwelling place of demons,**
> **a haunt of every foul and hateful bird,**
> **a haunt of every foul and hateful beast.**
> 3 **For all the nations have drunk of the wine of the wrath of her fornication,**
> **and the kings of the earth have committed fornication with her,**
> **and the merchants of the earth have grown rich from the power of her luxury."**

The destruction of Babylon had been predicted, but now the vision shows the effects of that destruction, not just the process. An angel tells John what has happened. This angel is different than the others, however, for it is described as having such radiance that the earth was made bright. This brightness is a sign of closeness to God. Indeed, this angel is said to have "great authority" (18:1), evidently even more than the previous angels had. Other angels have spoken with "loud voices" (5:2; 7:2; 14:7, 9, 15, 18; 16:17), but this one speaks with a "mighty voice" (18:2). This greater authority may be in the messenger, but it may be the message itself that makes the difference. The end of Babylon has come. Now the earth is being freed from her power. Yet the message is very negative for Babylon, even if it is good news for the faithful followers of God.

The description of fallen Babylon bears a great resemblance to Jeremiah's depiction of doom on ancient Babylon, especially Jeremiah 50:39 and 51:37. The sign of the total destruction of the city is that wild animals now live in the ruins. It is no longer fit for human habitation. In Revelation 18:2 it is said that Babylon has become the home of hateful birds and beasts. In Jeremiah 50:39 the description is more specific: hyenas and ostriches dwell in the city; in Jeremiah 51:37, it is said to be a den of jackals. In John's vision, even demons now join the wild animals in the deserted city.

Ancient cities could give the appearance of permanence. But their life was dependent on the ability to bring food into the city from a distance— even a great distance if the city were very large—and therefore economic and military control of vast areas was necessary. If those conditions changed, cities could be depopulated very rapidly. In addition, disease could take its toll, especially if the population had been weakened through famine.

The city of Rome, John's Babylon, was such a mighty and powerful city. It did control the economic life of vast areas and therefore could survive. At its height, about John's time, it had a population of about one million. By the sixth century, after the defeat of its armies, the loss of its economic base, and the effects of invasion, famine, and disease, the city of Rome had only about 30,000 inhabitants. In such a situation, it would not be at all surprising to find that wild animals had come well within the old city limits, now abandoned by human beings.

It is very important to see the connection between the economic power of a city, especially a city that is the capital of an empire, and the ease with which the city can be destroyed when its economic power is gone. It is also important to realize the degree to which economic power and military power are related. When economic power is gone, there is no money for armies. When military power is gone, economic security cannot be guaranteed. John's vision indicated that Babylon would lose its military power, because the ten kings of the earth would manage to turn against the empire. Her economic collapse inevitably would follow. Revelation 18:3 stresses that both the kings of the earth and the merchants have been involved in Rome's prosperity. They will also be affected by her demise.

THE CALL TO THE FAITHFUL
Revelation 18:4–8

18:4 **Then I heard another voice from heaven saying,**
"Come out of her, my people,
so that you do not take part in her sins,
and so that you do not share in her plagues;
5 **for her sins are heaped high as heaven,**
and God has remembered her iniquities.
6 **Render to her as she herself has rendered,**
and repay her double for her deeds;
mix a double draught for her in the cup she mixed.
7 **As she gloried herself and lived luxuriously,**
so give her a like measure of torment and grief.
Since in her heart she says,
'I rule as a queen;
I am no widow,
and I will never see grief,'
8 **therefore her plagues will come in a single day—**
pestilence and mourning and famine—
and she will be burned with fire;
for mighty is the Lord God who judges her."

The form of address changes. Until now, the vision had been focused on Babylon. Now it turns to the faithful. As is typical of visions, the time sequence is not clear. A different angel calls for the faithful to leave Babylon before the destruction occurs. Yet the previous chapters assumed that the faithful were present while the destruction was going on and were called to remain faithful in spite of the terrible events. Perhaps it is only this final destruction, so complete that few survive, that marks the time for the departure of the faithful. It is also not clear where they would go, since most of the known world was caught up in the imperial system.

The words are similar to those used by Jeremiah and by the prophet of the last part of Isaiah, both dealing with the end of the Babylonian exile in the sixth century B.C. Jeremiah writes: "Come out of her, my people! Save your lives, each of you, from the fierce anger of the LORD!" (Jer. 51:45). In Isaiah 48:20 we read: "Go out from Babylon, flee from Chaldea, declare this with a shout of joy, proclaim it, send it forth to the end of the earth; say, 'The LORD has redeemed his servant Jacob!' " The destruction of Babylon is the redemption of God's people.

The time of destruction is at hand. "God has remembered her iniquities" (18:5). This does not mean that God had forgotten them earlier or that God had been preoccupied with other matters. Rather, God had overlooked them, not dealt with them, because at that time they served God's purpose for exposing who the faithful were and who the opponents of God were. Now that time of testing is over. Choices have been made. The time for repentance has gone. Judgment has been made, and now the guilty ones face their punishment.

The call for God's people to leave a city before it is destroyed in judgment also bears a resemblance to the call for Lot and his family to leave Sodom before that city was destroyed. Similarly, angels brought the warning of the impending disaster (Gen. 19:12–23).

It is not clear to whom 18:6 is addressed. As it stands, it appears that the faithful are to repay Babylon for her evil deeds, but that is unlikely. Not only are they told to leave Babylon, but throughout the whole vision, the faithful have been encouraged to follow the way of the cross. Surely it is God who will avenge the faithful, through whatever agents God decides to use. The words may therefore be addressed to such agents. Babylon is to receive double the pain and suffering she has inflicted on others, drinking twice the amount of wine from the cup of God's wrath as others receive, since Babylon has been the leader of those who have done evil.

There is an ironic contrast between 18:7–8 and 17:4. In the earlier description of Babylon, the city is rich and powerful, with luxurious dress and jewels and with the trappings of royalty. Her punishment will be the removal of such grandeur. The one who said: "I rule as a queen" and did not believe her power could come to an end, will become like the despised widow, the one who has no one to intercede for her, the one who is grief-stricken and powerless in the society. The words are carefully chosen: Rome, John's Babylon, had glorified herself rather than the true God. Now she will be reviled and have nothing. Her pride as well as her evil deeds will be punished. There is a connection: Her pride let her believe she could do anything, that she was accountable to no one, and that led her to commit atrocities.

The conclusion of this word of judgment is also ironic. Rome had viewed herself as "The Eternal City"—indestructible. Yet it will take only a day for her to be destroyed (18:8). Rome thought of herself as the mightiest city, answerable to no one. But God is the one who is mighty, and it is God who is her judge. Whether she chooses to be or not, she is answerable to God.

BABYLON'S MOURNERS
Revelation 18:9–19

> 18:9 And the kings of the earth, who committed fornication and lived in luxury with her, will weep and wail over her when they see the smoke of her burning; [10] they will stand far off, in fear of her torment, and say,
> "Alas, alas, the great city,
> Babylon, the mighty city!
> For in one hour your judgment has come."
> [11] And the merchants of the earth weep and mourn for her, since no one buys their cargo anymore, [12] cargo of gold, silver, jewels and pearls, fine linen, purple, silk and scarlet, all kinds of scented wood, all articles of ivory, all articles of costly wood, bronze, iron, and marble, [13] cinnamon, spice, incense, myrrh, frankincense, wine, olive oil, choice flour and wheat, cattle and sheep, horses and chariots, slaves—and human lives.
> [14] "The fruit for which your soul longed
> has gone from you,
> and all your dainties and your splendor
> are lost to you, never to be found again!"
> [15] The merchants of these wares, who gained wealth from her, will stand far off, in fear of her torment, weeping and mourning aloud,
> [16] "Alas, alas, the great city,
> clothed in fine linen, in purple and scarlet,
> adorned with gold, with jewels, and with pearls!
> [17] For in one hour all this wealth has been laid waste!" And all shipmasters and seafarers, sailors and all whose trade is on the sea, stood far off [18] and cried out as they saw the smoke of her burning,
> "What city was like the great city?"
> [19] And they threw dust on their heads, as they wept and mourned, crying out,
> "Alas, alas, the great city,
> where all who had ships at sea grew rich by her wealth!
> For in one hour she has been laid waste."

This section is very dramatic. There are similarities between this part of the vision and one in Ezekiel that foretold the destruction of Tyre (Ezekiel 26–27). Visualize the scene in Revelation 18. The great city is destroyed. Around the ruins three choruses are standing. These are not Romans, but rather those who had profited from the success of the empire. The first chorus is made up of the kings of the earth (18:9), that group allied earlier with Rome. The second is made up of merchants (18:11) from all over the world who had made a profit from their trade with Rome. The third is composed of seamen (18:17) who transported the goods from the four corners of the earth. In each case, they stand at some distance, fearful of danger to themselves (18:10, 15, 17), chanting dirges as they watch the city burn. In each case, their laments end with words about the swiftness of the judgment upon the city, in only one hour (18:10, 17, 19). These three groups—kings, merchants, and seamen—all relied on Rome for their own success. Her fall means disruption, insecurity, and even failure for themselves.

The first group, the kings, are specifically those kings whose own lives of luxury were related to Rome's success. They have the least to say of all the groups. Perhaps they will remain secure in their own kingdoms; perhaps they will have greater independence now. Perhaps they are fearful that they themselves may suffer the same judgment in the future. But their mourning makes clear that they have lost a friend.

The second group, the merchants, are much more specific about what they have lost. They have goods to sell, but no one will buy them now. No one has money for such things. The good life is gone. The list of their wares is informative: luxury items of gold and silver, jewels and pearls, fine fabrics of linen and silk, fine dyes of purple and scarlet—all things worn by the woman personifying Rome described in 17:4. There are luxury items for homes: scented woods, bronze, iron, and marble. There are luxury ingredients for the table: cinnamon, spice, wine, olive oil, fine flour, cattle, and sheep. There are other luxury items: incense, myrrh, frankincense, horses, and chariots. Last on the list are slaves—human beings bought and sold as merchandise. The regret of the merchants is that no one buys these things anymore. But the list as a whole, with its great luxuries, and the final entry of slaves, points to the evil in which both Rome and the merchants were involved. The slaves may have been those captured in battle. They may also have been the poor who could no longer pay their debts and had to sell themselves or their children into slavery (18:12–13).

The lament sung by the merchants is to the point: All the things for which Rome longed are now gone from her forever. This is true in two ways. First, since the luxurious lifestyle she longed for above all was in itself sinful, because it involved an economic system that led to misery for many, judgment has taken from her all of those luxuries. Second, even if the things she longed for had not been evil, but rather quite neutral, to have them as the center of one's life is to invite disaster, for they are not worthy of our highest love. The words of Jesus apply here: we should seek first the kingdom of God and God's righteousness (Matt. 6:33).

The text goes on to describe the fear of the merchants, which causes them to stand at some distance. Perhaps their fear is caused by their own involvement in Rome's evil, and therefore there is the possibility of their own judgment. The lament of the merchants rehearses the fine way in which the city had been dressed, using the same description of the whore as in 17:4 and closing with the refrain that all her wealth had been taken from her in one hour (18:17).

The third group, the seamen, are a mixed group, including the owners of the ships as well as the sailors. They all had become rich by trade with Rome (18:19), carrying all the things the merchants sold, including slaves. Without Rome, their wealth has gone as well. Because no one can buy the luxury goods the merchants used to sell, there is no need for transportation.

The seamen are a very important group. The Roman Empire had made the Mediterranean Sea a private lake of the empire, for it controlled all the surrounding land areas, from Gibraltar to the Holy Land. The empire had used its military might to clear the area of pirates, so that shipping by sea was the easiest and cheapest way to transport goods for long distances. The only problem might be the weather. When the western half of the Roman Empire fell in the fifth century, one of the results was the increasing insecurity of travel on the sea. There was also a great loss of wealth in the West and therefore little commerce other than very local. It would not be until the twelfth century or so before the kind of luxury goods the merchants mentioned in 18:12–13 would appear again in the markets of western Europe.

THE JOYOUS CHORUS
Revelation 18:20–24

18:20 **"Rejoice over her, O heaven, you saints and apostles and prophets!**
For God has given judgment for you against her."

21 **Then a mighty angel took up a stone like a great millstone and threw it into the sea, saying,**

　"With such violence Babylon the great city
　　will be thrown down,
　　and will be found no more;
22 **and the sound of harpists and minstrels and of flutists and trumpeters**
　　will be heard in you no more;
　and an artisan of any trade will be found in you no more; and the sound of the millstone will be heard in you no more;
23 **and the light of a lamp will shine in you no more;**
　　and the voice of bridegroom and bride will be heard in you no more;
　for your merchants were the magnates of the earth,
　　and all nations were deceived by your sorcery.
24 **And in you was found the blood of prophets and of saints,**
　　and of all who have been slaughtered on earth."

It is not said whose voices the words belong to in 18:20. Clearly it is not any of the mourners whose final lament is in 18:19. This is a different voice and a different mood. While the kings, the merchants, and the seamen mourn, this voice calls for saints and apostles and prophets—the faithful—to rejoice. Now their great persecutor, the one who constantly tried to seduce them into idolatry and other sins, has been destroyed. Not only has Babylon been judged, but so have the saints, and the judgment is for them, against Babylon.

Another angel appears on the scene, evidently while the three choruses of mourners watch the city burn, and the heavenly chorus watches in a very different mood. This angel picks up a great stone and throws it into the sea. This may well be based on the words of Jesus recorded in the Synoptic Gospels: that any who put a stumbling block in the way of discipleship for one of the little ones might better have a millstone put around his neck and be thrown into the sea (Matt. 18:6; Mark 9:42; Luke 17:2). Rome has definitely put many stumbling blocks in the path of the faithful, so the angel says that Babylon will be thrown into the sea.

The angel continues with a description of all the good things in life that will no longer be part of life in Babylon, the deserted and destroyed city: no musicians, no artisans, no mills, no lamplight, no joyful weddings. It is interesting to look at this list and to compare it to the list in 18:12–13. The previous list was composed of luxury items only the rich would have had the money to enjoy. This list, however, comprises the simple pleasures of ordinary life, enjoyed by all but the most destitute. One does not have to be rich to have musicians, though the wealthy can hire minstrels and trumpeters. Artisans of some form are a necessary part of life, though the wealthy may hire exquisite workers. Everyone needs millers, though the flour of the rich may be finer. Lamps of some sort light the homes of all people, though the rich may have better ones. And the joy of weddings is there for families of every level, though the form of the celebration would be different for the rich than for the poor. When a whole society goes astray, the judgment effects everyone.

The angel states that judgment has come partly because the merchants of Babylon had become very powerful and had corrupted those with whom they traded. The economic forces of Babylon were a major means by which their idolatry was exported. It was the very success of Rome, John's Babylon, that led other nations to ally themselves with her and to integrate their economies with hers. Therefore, other nations and their merchants followed the idolatrous way of Rome, holding her in highest regard, doing what pleased her, and thereby corrupting themselves. Had Rome been a weak or poor nation, there would not have been such temptation to imitate or follow her. Rome's success as an economic power was a major factor leading to the judgment God rendered upon her. Economic success is not a reliable indicator of virtue.

The final word of the angel is that Rome was in some sense responsible for the deaths of all of the saints and prophets. It even implies that all deaths by violence were caused by Babylon (18:24). As a historical reference, this is impossible, since there was a long time of such behavior before Rome even existed. What may be meant is that the basic character of the Roman Empire comprises the quest for power, the greed for luxuries that needs such power, the injustice that such greed creates, and the idolatry that perpetuates the search for unlimited power and its fruits. It is this complex of evil that murdered the prophets who had pointed to God's sovereignty and justice, and the saints who had lived by God's law. In that sense, Rome was the current embodiment of the beast—the political shape of evil that opposes God and leads human beings to do so.

10. The End of the Old
Revelation 19:1–20:15

THE JOYFUL RESPONSE OF HEAVEN
Revelation 19:1–5

19:1 **After this I heard what seemed to be the loud voice of a great multitude in heaven, saying,**

> **"Hallelujah!**
> **Salvation and glory and power to our God,**
> 2   **for his judgments are true and just;**
> **he has judged the great whore**
>   **who corrupted the earth with her fornication,**
> **and he has avenged on her the blood of his servants."**

3 **Once more they said,**

> **"Hallelujah!**
> **The smoke goes up from her forever and ever."**

4 **And the twenty-four elders and the four living creatures fell down and worshiped God who is seated on the throne, saying,**

> **"Amen. Hallelujah!"**

5 **And from the throne came a voice saying,**

> **"Praise our God, all you his servants,**
> **and all who fear him, small and great."**

Revelation 18 closed with words of condemnation and destruction of Babylon/Rome. Chapter 19 opens on a very different note—one of joy and victory. Yet the two are clearly related; only the perspective has changed. Precisely because of the destruction of Babylon, heaven can rejoice. Not just a few voices sing, but many. When Revelation speaks of "a great multitude," it refers not only to the angels and heavenly hosts but also to the saints—those who have followed God faithfully on earth, those martyred because of their faith. The content of the hymn sung by this great multitude gives great praise to God. In fact, the saints are called saints precisely because they chose to praise God instead of praising Babylon. When Babylon is destroyed, the major alternative to praising God is gone.

The saints, along with the heavenly host, praise God's justice. The destruction of Babylon is an act of justice, because Babylon had killed the saints, and the destruction of Babylon is the avenging of their blood. Part of the gospel message is the word of the cross. The saints did not avenge themselves. They suffered and died, apparently in weakness. They had lived as Paul encouraged Christians to do: "Beloved, never avenge yourselves, but leave room for the wrath of God" (Rom. 12:19). Now God's wrath has come, and it is an act of justice. However strange it may seem at first, if there were no wrath and no justice, then the praise of God would not be complete. There would still be opposition from the Babylons of the earth.

It is not only the saints who sing "hallelujah." Revelation 19:4 continues the description of this act of praise. The twenty-four elders and four living creatures, already introduced in John's vision, continue their worship at the throne of God (see 4:4–8). Their words make clear that this praise is taking place at the throne of God. The voice from the throne then urges the continuation of praise by the saints, "both the small and great." This evidently refers to those saints who were well-known martyrs and those who were faithful in less spectacular ways.

THE BRIDE AND THE WEDDING FEAST
Revelation 19:6–10

19:6 Then I heard what seemed to be the voice of a great multitude, like the sound of many waters and like the sound of mighty thunderpeals, crying out,
"Hallelujah!
For the Lord our God the Almighty reigns.
7 Let us rejoice and exult and give him the glory,
for the marriage of the Lamb has come,
and his bride has made herself ready;
8 to her it has been granted to be clothed
with fine linen, bright and pure"—
for the fine linen is the righteous deeds of the saints.
9 And the angel said to me, "Write this: Blessed are those who are invited to the marriage supper of the Lamb." And he said to me, "These are true words of God." 10 Then I fell down at his feet to worship him, but he said to me, "You must not do that! I am a fellow servant with you and your comrades who hold the testimony of Jesus. Worship God! For the testimony of Jesus is the spirit of prophecy."

The narrative moves forward in these verses. Briefly, but significantly, John has a glimpse of the victory beyond Babylon: the future uncorrupted by sin. What will happen after vengeance, after the destruction of Babylon and all of God's enemies? Does something new and positive lie ahead once all this warfare has ended? Verses 6 through 10 give voice to this tantalizing vision, and then the reader is taken back to the time of the final destruction of sin and its embodiments.

Who is speaking? This probably is the collective voice of the great multitude mentioned in 19:1. It announces not only God's victory but, beyond that, the marriage of the Lamb. The Lamb is to marry the bride. The Lamb has already been identified as Christ (see especially Rev. 5:6–14). The bride is about to be identified as those faithful to Christ, that is, the church.

The imagery of the people of God as the bride of God is frequent in scripture. This is why the imagery of the harlot had such power: It was the opposite of the faithfulness that the covenant of marriage and the covenant with God demand. In the New Testament, Paul speaks of the church in Corinth as the bride he is preparing for Christ (2 Cor. 11:2). Ephesians 5:23–32 uses the imagery of the bride as well. The bride of Christ is the antithesis of the great whore. They are distinguished by their loves and their alliances. They are also distinguished by their dress. Whereas the harlot had been dressed to entice others to sin, the bride is dressed in "fine linen, bright and pure"; this linen is composed of "the righteous deeds of the saints." These righteous deeds are the way in which "the bride has made herself ready." Both the harlot and the bride are corporate, even though they are images of individuals.

The symbolism of the wedding feast is also significant because it points to a new level of union that has been promised but has not yet taken place. It also indicates the intimacy and permanence of the union that is to follow the feast.

The reader is reminded that John is receiving a vision when the voice of an angel speaks, telling John to write down some specific words and the description of what he is seeing and hearing. The words are very interesting: "Blessed are those who are invited to the marriage supper of the Lamb." This statement is followed by the claim that "These are true words of God" (19:9). The beatitude is not simply the opinion of the angel. Rather, it is God's own blessing on those who are invited to this wedding feast. Two points are made in these few words. First, no one comes to this heavenly banquet without an invitation. Second, to be invited is a great blessing. Those who are invited are those who are part of the bride, whose righteous deeds form the dress for the wedding.

The imagery of the wedding feast is frequent in the gospels, and the overtones of the parables that use it are heard in this passage. Most significant is the parable in Matthew 22:1–14, where those first invited to the wedding banquet refuse to come, and so others are invited. But when these others arrive, they are not wearing wedding garments, and are condemned. Here, in John's vision, those invited are those who have contributed to the wedding garment of the bride precisely by their righteous actions.

John is so astonished by this proclamation that he falls down at the feet of the angel in order to worship him. Heavenly beings had spoken to him before, but John had not sought to respond in this way. What is different here is the presence of the Word of God, delivered by the angel. Even so, the angel responds that he is not to be worshiped, but rather he is a servant of God, just as John and his fellow Christians are. All of them are to maintain their witness to Jesus. God only is to be worshiped. Those who bear the message of Jesus are not to be worshiped.

But those who do faithfully bear witness to Jesus are authentic prophets. The spirit of prophecy cannot be separated from the faithful witness to Jesus. Prophets who declare that which is in opposition to the true testimony about Jesus are not true prophets. The spirit of prophecy is tied to the message about Jesus that John and the Christian community are proclaiming.

THE RIDER ON THE WHITE HORSE
Revelation 19:11–16

19:11 **Then I saw heaven opened, and there was a white horse! Its rider is called Faithful and True, and in righteousness he judges and makes war. 12 His eyes are like a flame of fire, and on his head are many diadems; and he has a name inscribed that no one knows but himself. 13 He is clothed in a robe dipped in blood, and his name is called The Word of God. 14 And the armies of heaven, wearing fine linen, white and pure, were following him on white horses. 15 From his mouth comes a sharp sword with which to strike down the nations, and he will rule them with a rod of iron; he will tread the winepress of the fury of the wrath of God the Almighty. 16 On his robe and on his thigh he has a name inscribed, "King of kings and Lord of lords."**

The pleasant interlude ends, and there is a return to the destruction and to the scene of battle. The figure on a white horse comes from heaven in order to fight the beast. Clearly this is the figure of Christ. He is given many names in this brief passage: "Faithful and True," "The Word of God," and "The King of kings and Lord of lords" (19:11, 13, 16). But he is also said to have a name that no one knows (19:12). The meaning of this passage is not clear. His name is Jesus, but is that name to be revealed to all at the end? Is there another name yet to be revealed? There is a hint of this in 3:12, where Jesus promises that those who remain faithful will have written on them the name of God, the name of the city of God, and Jesus' own new name.

The figure on the white horse is crowned with many diadems, more than enough to take on the beast who also has ten diadems (13:1; 19:12). His eyes are like those of the figure of Christ who appeared in the beginning of John's vision (1:14). His robe is dipped in blood, and it is said that he will tread the winepress of God's wrath—the same image that appeared in 14:19–20 in the prophecy of the destruction of the earth. He alone is the one who can destroy the powers of evil.

It is important to note the weapon with which the rider on the white horse will conquer the beast: the sword from the mouth of the one who is the Word of God. The imagery of the Word of God as a sword appears frequently in the New Testament, both in John's vision and elsewhere. It is used three times before in Revelation: (1) in 1:16, Jesus is described as having a two-edged sword coming from his mouth; (2) in 2:12, the message to the church at Pergamum describes Jesus as the one who has the two-edged sword; and (3) in 2:16, the message to the same church warns that Jesus will come to make war on them with the two-edged sword. In Ephesians 6:17, Christians are told to take "the sword of the Spirit, which is the word of God." Hebrews 4:12 spells out even more clearly the power of this sword: "Indeed, the word of God is living and active, sharper than any two-edged sword, piercing until it divides soul from spirit, joints from marrow; it is able to judge the thoughts and intentions of the heart."

The only weapon that matters is the Word of God. Horses and chariots, armies and weapons of mass destruction, economic and political power of all sorts: These come to nothing before the Word of God. The weapons of Babylon seem terrible, but they cannot ultimately withstand the power of the Word of God. The faithful suffering in Asia Minor, who feared more persecution might come, are encouraged to stand fast with the Word of God and not to fear the weapons that Rome can use against them. In this they are reminded of the words of Jesus in Matthew 10:28: "Do not fear those who kill the body but cannot kill the soul; rather fear him who can destroy both soul and body in hell." A single rider, the one who is the Word of God, can defeat all the armies of Babylon. He is "the King of kings and the Lord of lords" (19:16).

THE OTHER BANQUET
Revelation 19:17–21

> 19:17 **Then I saw an angel standing in the sun, and with a loud voice he called to all the birds that fly in midheaven, "Come, gather for the great supper of God,** [18] **to eat the flesh of kings, the flesh of captains, the flesh of the mighty, the flesh of horses and their riders—flesh of all, both free and slave, both small and great."** [19] **Then I saw the beast and the kings of the earth with their armies gathered to make war against the rider on the horse and against his army.** [20] **And the beast was captured, and with it the false prophet who had performed in its presence the signs by which he deceived those who had received the mark of the beast and those who worshiped its image. These two were thrown alive into the lake of fire that burns with sulfur.** [21] **And the rest were killed by the sword of the rider on the horse, the sword that came from his mouth; and all the birds were gorged with their flesh.**

While the saints are invited to the marriage feast of the Lamb, another banquet is scheduled. This is a terrible feast that no human would wish to attend. The invitation is issued by an angel in midheaven to birds of prey. The food for the feast is the bodies of the kings and captains, and horses and armies, of those who have gathered to fight against the rider on the white horse. This vision has parallels in the vision Ezekiel had of the destruction of the enemies of Israel before the creation of the new temple (Ezek. 39:17–20). In that vision, God commands Ezekiel to invite the birds and wild animals to such a feast.

Very quickly, the battle occurs. The beast is captured, along with its image, the focus of its worship by human beings. Both of these are thrown into the lake of fire. The rest of the armies, now that their true leader has been captured, fall quickly and are destroyed. The birds then come to eat the flesh of the fallen.

In Revelation 17–19, there are parallels between the great whore and the bride of the Lamb, and between the feast of the birds on the flesh of the defeated armies and the wedding feast of the Lamb. Those who follow the great whore will go to the terrible feast of the birds. Those who follow the Lamb will go to the blessed wedding feast as part of the bride. The message for John's readers is to remain faithful so that they will be part of the good feast. They are also consoled with the word that the ones who seem so powerful, the ones who can persecute them, will be destroyed.

THE MILLENNIUM
Revelation 20:1–3

> 20:1 **Then I saw in angel coming down from heaven, holding in his hand the key to the bottomless pit and a great chain. 2 He seized the dragon, that ancient serpent, who is the Devil and Satan, and bound him for a thousand years, 3 and threw him into the pit, and locked and sealed it over him, so that he would deceive the nations no more, until the thousand years were ended. After that he must be let out for a little while.**

Revelation 20 contains some of the strangest portions of the book. This chapter provides a description of the thousand-year period where evil powers are repressed, a time period known as the *millennium*. Christ reigns during this period, along with the martyrs who have been raised from the dead in the first of two resurrections.

Christians have often debated about the exact meaning and time of the millennium. Some believe that the millennium began with the resurrection of Christ and that we are now living in this thousand-year period. Others believe that the passage refers to a thousand years of peace before the Second Coming of Christ—a time that has not yet begun. Still others believe that the millennium follows the Second Coming.

In Revelation, after the thousand-year period is over, the power of evil is unleashed. Then comes the final battle, the dragon, and the resurrection and final judgment of all human beings take place. This is a complex chapter and must be dealt with in detail in fairly brief sections.

The beast and its image have been destroyed. But the dragon, the power behind the other manifestations of evil, still remains. Now the dragon is captured and put out of commission for a thousand years. This is an interim of peace, before the devil is released from captivity and allowed to be active again for a brief time.

But John's vision does not provide a clear calendar. What is important for him, and for the Christians to whom he writes, is that a time will come when evil apparently will be overcome. Yet the ultimate source of that evil—the dragon, or Satan—is not completely destroyed. There is no thought here that God could not have overcome evil all at once. It somehow serves God's purpose to permit this interlude of peace, this time without evil, and then allow evil again to hold sway. What will Christians do if the persecution ceases and if there is no opposition to the church? Will Christians forget to be faithful in such times of peace? What will happen if there is a long time of peace, and then the dragon is let loose again, however briefly? Will Christians who have been used to the good times remain faithful? That is part of the issue here, even as it was part of the issue in the letters to the church at Sardis (3:1–6) and at Laodicea (3:14–22).

The millennium is pictured as part of the history of this world, here on earth. The vision implies that the new earth will not become a reality until there is a redeemed old earth, which is what occurs during this thousand-year break in the power of evil. The power of evil lessens, and redemption begins its work, to be completed by the transformation of the world at the end of history. This is a much more optimistic view of history than one that sees evil having full sway until the end, with no time on this earth when evil is in abeyance.

THE TWO RESURRECTIONS
Revelation 20:4–6

20:4 **Then I saw thrones, and those seated on them were given authority to judge. I also saw the souls of those who had been beheaded for their testimony to Jesus and for the word of God. They had not worshiped the beast or its image and had not received its mark on their foreheads or their hands. They came to life and reigned with Christ a thousand years.** 5 **(The rest of the dead did not come to life until the thousand years were ended.) This is the first resurrection.** 6 **Blessed and holy are those who share in the first resurrection. Over these the second death has no power, but they will be priests of God and of Christ, and they will reign with him a thousand years.**

The chapter continues with further description of the thousand years before the final destruction of the dragon. It speaks of two distinct resurrections. In the first resurrection, the martyrs who died for their faith—here specifically spoken of as those who had been beheaded—are raised to rule with Christ during the thousand years. Those who had been beheaded are only a small portion of the martyrs. (Roman citizens convicted of capital crimes were often beheaded; others were given more gruesome executions.) Thus, these martyrs represent only a small portion of the faithful.

Who exactly is raised at this point? If they are all the faithful, then who is to be raised at the second resurrection? Are they only the martyrs who died before the millennium and not the faithful who come during the thousand years? John does not answer the questions that immediately come to our minds, for his is not a specifically drawn blueprint. He does wish to make clear that the martyrs will be vindicated. Their faithfulness has been established, and they will suffer no further testing. They are ready to reign with Christ when the time comes. They fulfill their role as the priestly people during this time. Others are not yet ready for such a role. They have not yet been raised and will not be until the thousand years are over and the dragon is again let loose. Does that mean that they could again face testing and fall away? Such questions are not answered by this text.

What is the character of this peaceful interlude? The idea of a thousand-year reign of Christ with the saints before the end of history has little currency in the rest of biblical literature. In fact, the thousand years spoken of in this passage often have been interpreted in a very different way. For instance, in the fourth century Augustine assumed that there had been six thousand years of human history before Christ and that the thousand years spoken of here began with the birth of Jesus. This interpretation meant that history would end in the year 1000, with the thousand years being the time of the church. Medieval Christians believed this interpretation, and as the year 1000 approached, there was great consternation that the final judgment was about to begin and that history would end. It is no wonder that after 1000, when life went on, there was great rejoicing and a sense of renewal. Part of the rationale for this was that history was seen as involving a gigantic week: six days of a thousand years each, plus one day—a sabbath—of one thousand years. The year 2000 raises some of the same questions, so it is not surprising that there has been a renewed interest in issues of the millennium.

The idea of two resurrections is also rare in biblical or early Christian literature. There are several issues involved here. It is clear that those who are *in* Christ cannot be separated from him by death. We know that the idea that when people die their souls go directly to heaven, and that heavenly life is life eternal, is not biblical in origin. The Bible speaks rather of an eternal life whose fullness comes with the resurrection of the body. Yet the notion of a time between a Christians's death and resurrection seems to involve a separation from Christ that is quite unacceptable.

In the book of Revelation, the martyrs are already in heaven, although they are not yet enjoying the fullness of eternal life. (The passage dealing with the opening of the fifth seal [6:9–11] shows the souls of the martyrs under the altar in heaven, where they are told to rest a while longer. This evidently takes place before their resurrection.) Rather than try to develop a clear calendar of future events, perhaps we should simply trust that fu-

ture to the One who has created time and eternity, and whose love has
been revealed in Jesus Christ.

THE FINAL CONFLICT
Revelation 20:7–10

> 20:7 **When the thousand years are ended, Satan will be released from his
> prison** [8] **and will come out to deceive the nations at the four corners of the
> earth, Gog and Magog, in order to gather them for battle; they are as nu-
> merous as the sands of the sea.** [9] **They marched up over the breadth of the
> earth and surrounded the camp of the saints and the beloved city. And fire
> came down from heaven and consumed them.** [10] **And the devil who had de-
> ceived them was thrown into the lake of fire and sulfur, where the beast and
> the false prophet were, and they will be tormented day and night forever
> and ever.**

When Satan is released, many follow him. Gog and Magog are frequently
mentioned in Jewish apocalyptic literature. In Ezekiel 38:2, Gog is referred to as "the chief prince of Meshech and Tubal" of the land of Magog. In Ezekiel's vision, when Israel is crushed by the Exile, the prophet
is given the vision of the Valley of Dry Bones, indicating the resurrection
of the nation (Ezekiel 37). In the vision, after this resurrection, Gog leads
an invasion against the renewed Israel. Ezekiel 38—39 describe the battle
and destruction of Gog and Magog, complete with the invitation to the
birds to consume the flesh of the fallen (Ezek. 39:17–20), as mentioned in
Revelation 19:17–21.

Evil does not die quickly. Even the thousand years of peace have not
ended the ease with which some will follow Satan when he makes his appearance. Revelation 20:8 says that the followers of Gog and Magog are
as numerous as the sands of the sea. Satan deceives the nations at the corners of the earth. This may seem a strange description, but it is leading to
a very important symbolic point. There is a center of the earth, and there
are four corners. The camp of the saints is in the beloved city (20:9), which
is at the center. The armies that march against it come from the corners.
The beloved city is Jerusalem, whose heavenly transformation will be seen
in the next chapter.

There is no real battle. The armies of Gog and Magog gather around
the saints, who are in the beloved city. Fire comes down from heaven and
kills all the evil ones. At that point, the devil joins the beast and the false
prophet in the lake of fire forever.

THE FINAL JUDGMENT
Revelation 20:11–15

> 20:11 **Then I saw a great white throne and the one who sat on it; the earth and the heaven fled from his presence, and no place was found for them.** ¹² **And I saw the dead, great and small, standing before the throne, and books were opened. Also another book was opened, the book of life. And the dead were judged according to their works, as recorded in the books.** ¹³ **And the sea gave up the dead that were in it, Death and Hades gave up the dead that were in them, and all were judged according to what they had done.** ¹⁴ **Then Death and Hades were thrown into the lake of fire. This is the second death, the lake of fire;** ¹⁵ **and anyone whose name was not found written in the book of life was thrown into the lake of fire.**

There have been so many almost-final struggles, after which evil has come back to plague this world. When the real end comes, however, it is described in very brief terms. Yet these few verses describe the goal of all else that has gone before and lead the way to the fulfillment of all the promises given to the faithful. All that John sees now is God on the throne, radiant in purity. When the throne is mentioned earlier in the vision, it is usually surrounded by the twenty-four elders and the four living creatures. The One on the throne was the object of their worship (see especially chaps. 4 and 5). Now, however, there are no elders, no living creatures, no earth, and no heaven. All are gone. Only God on the throne remains. The time of judgment is at hand. The disappearance of the earth may be expected at the end of history, but the disappearance of heaven is unexpected. Yet heaven is as much the creation of God as is the earth, and God is beyond all creation. Even those who are part of the first resurrection are not in this vision. All will have to be renewed when the judgment is over. All will be part of a new creation, beyond judgment.

The dead come to life again in order to be judged. All of the dead come before the throne. No one can assume that they were so insignificant that their actions do not matter. Both "great and small" are judged. Those who were buried in the sea cannot escape judgment. Death loses its control over the departed. Hades, the place condemnation, also loses its power. Those held by the sea, by Death, and by Hades all now appear to be judged.

Is this the second resurrection? John does not call it that. It is an appearance before the throne, a recalling from death for that purpose, but it does not necessarily lead to eternal life. The term "resurrection" usually has this positive connotation, which is missing here. All that is said at this point is that all who have died are to be judged at the end of history. And God is the sole judge.

On what basis are the dead to be judged? On the basis of the contents of books. It would be easy to assume that there are two books: one filled with accounts of evil actions; the other filled with accounts of good actions. But the situation is not that simple. Revelation 20:12 states that "books were opened" as the judgment begins. Then it adds that "another book" was opened, the book of life.

The phrase "the book of life" occurs only once outside the book of Revelation. That is in Paul's letter to the Philippians where he refers to his co-workers as those "whose names are in the book of life" (Phil. 4:3). The phrase occurs six times in Revelation: three times before chapter 20, twice in chapter 20, and once in chapter 21. In 3:5, Jesus speaks as the one who is able to remove a name from the book of life. In 13:8, that book is spoken of as "the book of life of the Lamb that was slaughtered." In 17:8, those whose names are not in the book of life are astonished at the appearance of the beast.

In these last two instances, the names in the book are said to have been there from the foundation of the world. The book of life is not a list of good deeds done by various people. Nor is it a list of names of those who have done more good than evil. Morality, as such, is not the immediate basis of the judgment. In the presence of the holy God, no creature can be counted perfectly righteous. The book of life has to do with faith in and faithfulness to Jesus. Those who have faith in Jesus have repented and received forgiveness. They have conquered because they have followed the One who has conquered all evil. This is not "cheap grace," however. Faithfulness in their earthly lives meant following Jesus rather than the way of the beast. Such faithfulness could lead to great suffering and even death.

These brief verses are packed with important theological issues: the relation of faith and works, and of free will and grace. They affirm the importance of works, but faithfulness is central. Names are written in the Lamb's book of life from the foundation of the world, but Jesus is able to remove the faithless from such a list. What is made clear is that everyone's life will be laid open—nothing can be hidden from God's scrutiny. "The books" are filled with accounts of all that we have done, both good and evil. But beyond this reckoning is the book of life. Those whose names are there are the redeemed, whose evil deeds have been forgiven and whose faithfulness has sometimes been tested by fire.

The judgment includes the condemnation of Death and Hades. They are thrown into the lake of fire to join the beast, the false prophet, and the devil. The power of all of these has come completely to an end. John calls the lake of fire "the second death." The first death is the one all creatures face. From that death, true resurrection is possible. The martyrs have already received such resurrection, and they do not face this second death. But those judged at the end face the possibility of this second death, from which there is no resurrection. In the letter to the church in Smyrna, Jesus says: "Whoever conquers will not be harmed by the second death" (2:11). The devil and his agents, along with Death and Hades, have no future power because they have been cast into the lake of fire from which there is no escape. In 20:15, all those whose names are not in the book of life are also thrown into the lake of fire. How many are these? We are not told. What matters to the Christians who receive John's vision is that evil will end, finally and completely. What matters ultimately is to remain faithful to Jesus.

With evil gone, the stage has been set for the new creation.

11. The Glorious Future
Revelation 21:1–22:21

THE NEW CREATION
Revelation 21:1–4

21:1 **Then I saw a new heaven and a new earth; for the first heaven and the first earth had passed away, and the sea was no more.** 2 **And I saw the holy city, the new Jerusalem, coming down out of heaven from God, prepared as a bride adorned for her husband.** 3 **And I heard a loud voice from the throne saying,**
> **"See, the home of God is among mortals.**
> **He will dwell with them as their God;**
> **they will be his peoples,**
> **and God himself will be with them;**
> 4 **he will wipe every tear from their eyes.**
> **Death will be no more;**
> **mourning and crying and pain will be no more,**
> **for the first things have passed away."**

All of the destruction that has occurred, the final judgment, the end of the old earth and heaven—all have taken place for the purpose of making way for the new. John had received a tantalizing hint of what was to come when he was told of the marriage feast of the Lamb (19:6–9). Now he sees this new heaven and new earth (21:1). There is no sea in this new earth, for the sea was understood to be a place of danger. For someone exiled on an island, as was John, the sea was also the cause of separation from loved ones.

Christians often assume that the biblical view of the end of history includes the end of the earth, and then the redeemed enter an unchanged heaven. That, however, is based on a nonbiblical view that discounts the value of the earth. The biblical picture presented here is quite different in two ways. First, heaven itself is new. Second, there is a new earth, which is the habitation of the redeemed. In 2 Peter 3:13 there is a similar expectation. A new earth is part of the eschatological hope of Israel, that is, the hope for the final end of history. It can be seen in Isaiah 11:1–9 and

65:17–25 and in Ezekiel 40—48 in the vision of the new temple. In all of these, there was an earthly quality to the future hope. Paul included a similar expectation of a renewed earth in Romans 8:19–23.

The new earth includes the heavenly Jerusalem, the beloved city, which comes down from this new heaven to earth. In order to recapture some of the poignancy of that imagery, we must remember that at the time John was writing, the old Jerusalem had been destroyed by the Roman armies. Thus, he is not speaking of a new Jerusalem that will supersede the fallen one, but of a *new* Jerusalem that will be both the restoration of that city and something far greater.

The imagery is complex, for the city is said to be dressed as a bride, ready to meet her husband. The mix of the image of the Holy City and a woman putting on festive clothing is also found in Isaiah 52:1 and 61:10. The inhabitants of the city are the faithful. They are the bride of Christ, who is the Lamb. Just as the great whore represented Babylon/Rome, the evil city, so the bride represents the heavenly Jerusalem, the Holy City. The culmination of the union, the covenant, between God and the faithful people occurs in this marriage.

No longer will there be a great separation between heaven and earth. It is not so much that the redeemed shall be taken to heaven but rather that God will come among us and be part of the new Jerusalem. In the incarnation of Christ, God came among human beings as one of them, but still in a hidden fashion. Now, in this new creation, God will not be hidden, but will come among redeemed humanity in a direct, unmediated way.

Sin and evil have caused great suffering in the world. In the story of the fall in Genesis 3, death, pain, and suffering are the results of sin entering the human scene. In John's vision, once sin and evil have been completely conquered, these consequences will also be gone. It is God who has conquered sin, and therefore God is the one who will wipe away all the tears of those who have suffered and mourned (21:4). These words echo those of the elder when the sixth seal was opened (7:17) and the earlier prophecy of Isaiah (Isa. 25:8). The new creation lives out from under the cloud of death. It is eternal life. The old life has gone.

THE DIVISION OF FAITHFUL AND UNFAITHFUL
Revelation 21:5–8

21:5 **And the one who was seated on the throne said, "See, I am making all things new." Also he said, "Write this, for these words are trustworthy and** true." ⁶ Then he said to me, "It is done! I am the Alpha and the Omega, the beginning and the end. To the thirsty I will give water as a gift from the spring of the water of life. ⁷ Those who conquer will inherit these things, and I will be their God and they will be my children. ⁸ But as for the cowardly, the faithless, the polluted, the murderers, the fornicators, the sorcerers, the idolaters, and all liars, their place will be in the lake that burns with fire and sulfur, which is the second death."

It is not only that the old is gone. A new act of creation has taken place. God has created a new heaven and a new earth. This is still a vision, a glimpse of the future, but John sees these events as though they were happening before him. God speaks directly to John, telling him to write down the words that he is given. The throne has been understood to be the place of God, not the Lamb, but the words are reminiscent of the words spoken by the one "like the Son of Man" in 1:12, directing John to write. The work of redemption has been completed. The words: "It is done!" repeat the words of the seventh angel who poured out the last of the bowls of wrath (16:17). Evil has been defeated, and the way has been prepared for the new heaven and the new earth.

Only in Revelation are the terms "alpha" and "omega" used. In 1:8, God is described in this way. In 1:17, the one "like the Son of Man" describes himself as the first and the last. What is significant in this phrase, especially its use in 21:6, is the understanding that the whole work of creation and redemption, from beginning to end, is God's work and under God's providence. God was at the beginning; God is at the end. No strange god has determined the course of history. God's purposes from the beginning were this new heaven and new earth. Nothing, not even the forces of evil and the consequent sin and death, have been out from under God's providence. There was never an equal struggle between God and evil.

God promises to give water to the thirsty. It will not be ordinary water, but water "from the spring of the water of life." This parallels imagery used in the Gospel of John in the discussion of "living water" between Jesus and the woman at the well (John 4:14–15). In both cases, the water is the symbol of eternal life. This eternal life is the promised inheritance of those who remain faithful. With these words, which are a call to faithfulness, John and the readers are brought back to the realities of the old earth, the history in which the church is still suffering and evil is not yet destroyed. Those who conquer, who remain faithful in these difficult times, will become the children of God who are able to live in the city of God.

There are temptations to unfaithfulness. The list of sinful behaviors is interesting and shows the problems John saw in the churches (21:8). Those who cannot enter the city of God are those who are cowardly, who refuse to stand firm for the gospel in the midst of persecution. Condemned also are the faithless, who decide that the gospel is not true. The polluted may involve those who have been involved in collaboration with the beast, those who have tried to save their lives by submitting to the demands of the evil powers that hold sway over the earth until the final victory. All those who are not faithful, whose lives do not proclaim that Jesus is Lord, will suffer the second death and therefore will not take part in the inheritance of the saints, which is the Holy City.

THE NEW JERUSALEM
Revelation 21:9–21

21:9 **Then one of the seven angels who had the seven bowls full of the seven last plagues came and said to me, "Come, I will show you the bride, the wife of the Lamb."** [10] **And in the spirit he carried me away to a great, high mountain and showed me the holy city Jerusalem coming down out of heaven from God.** [11] **It has the glory of God and a radiance like a very rare jewel, like jasper, clear as crystal.** [12] **It has a great, high wall with twelve gates, and at the gates twelve angels, and on the gates are inscribed the names of the twelve tribes of the Israelites;** [13] **on the east three gates, on the north three gates, on the south three gates, and on the west three gates.** [14] **And the wall of the city has twelve foundations, and on them are the twelve names of the twelve apostles of the Lamb.**

[15] **The angel who talked to me had a measuring rod of gold to measure the city and its gates and walls.** [16] **The city lies foursquare, its length the same as its width; and he measured the city with his rod, fifteen hundred miles; its length and width and height are equal.** [17] **He also measured its wall, one hundred forty-four cubits by human measurement, which the angel was using.** [18] **The wall is built of jasper, while the city is pure gold, clear as glass.** [19] **The foundations of the wall of the city are adorned with every jewel; the first was jasper, the second sapphire, the third agate, the fourth emerald,** [20] **the fifth onyx, the sixth carnelian, the seventh chrysolite, the eighth beryl, the ninth topaz, the tenth chrysoprase, the eleventh jacinth, the twelfth amethyst.** [21] **And the twelve gates are twelve pearls, each of the gates is a single pearl, and the street of the city is pure gold, transparent as glass.**

It is significant that the angel who now addresses John to show him the bride of the Lamb is identified in the same way as the angel who showed him the great whore (17:1). The contrast between the two visions is clear. In the same way that the description of the great whore and the accompanying beast had been quite full, so the description of the city that is the bride is also very complete. The description has been influenced by Ezekiel's vision of the new temple (Ezekiel 40—48). In both cases, the seer is led by an angel who shows the new creation. The presence of the glory of God is central. In Ezekiel, that presence is made known because "the earth shone with his glory" (Ezek. 43:2). In John's vision, the presence of God's glory is seen in a "radiance like a very rare jewel, like a jasper, clear as crystal."

The number twelve figures prominently. There are twelve gates: three in each wall, with one of the names of the tribes of Israel carved on each. There are twelve foundations to the city wall, each with the name of one of the twelve apostles of Jesus. The connection between Israel and the church is clear: There is continuity between them. This was a very important issue in the life of the church, beginning about the time of John's vision. Had God completely rejected Israel and started again with a new people, a new redemption unrelated to Israel? John's answer is clear. The Christian gospel is integrated with the promises given to Israel and with the work of God in Israel. The Holy City is related both to the twelve tribes and to the twelve apostles.

If one takes seriously the dimensions given for the city, it is astonishing. The city is a cube: fifteen hundred miles in each direction, including its height. We cannot imagine what a city that size would look like. Are there buildings fifteen miles high? Is it the radiance of the glory of the city that is so high, with no particular structures involved? Obviously, it is an immense city, with room for an enormous number of inhabitants. The city is a corporate, social reality, and not just composed of individuals, each privately related to God.

In contrast to the immense size of the city, the walls are tiny: only a little more than two hundred feet high. Granted, in our current world a wall two hundred feet high would be surprising. In a city fifteen hundred miles high, however, such a wall is out of proportion. But for what reason does the heavenly city need a wall? It is more a line of demarcation than the defensive measure that historically has been the role of a city wall. The heavenly Jerusalem has no need of defense, for it has no enemies.

The picture of the city includes many references to gold and jewels. The city is beautiful and precious beyond all imagination. But the central imagery is the light, the radiance, the glory that is there because of the presence of God in the midst of the city. The city itself is made of gold so pure that it is as transparent as glass.

THE CITY WITHOUT A TEMPLE
Revelation 21:22–27

21:22 **I saw no temple in the city, for its temple is the Lord God the Almighty and the Lamb.** [23] **And the city has no need of sun or moon to shine on it, for the glory of God is its light, and its lamp is the Lamb.** [24] **The nations will walk by its light, and the kings of the earth will bring their glory into it.** [25] **Its gates will never be shut by day—and there will be no night there.** [26] **People will bring into it the glory and the honor of the nations.** [27] **But nothing unclean will enter it, nor anyone who practices abomination or falsehood, but only those who are written in the Lamb's book of life.**

The radical newness of this city of God is seen in 21:22–23. The city has no temple. The temple in Jerusalem was the promised place of God's presence among the people. Israel knew that God could not be contained in any human creation, but in Solomon's prayer of consecration for the original temple he prayed "that your eyes may be open night and day toward this house, the place of which you said, 'My name shall be there'" (1 Kings 8:29). The Temple was the place in which God's presence could be assured. Ezekiel, in a vision, saw the cloud of glory leave the Temple (Ezek. 10:18–19; 11:23) as a sign that God's presence had left the city and the Temple before they were destroyed. Ezekiel's vision of the restoration includes a new temple. John's vision does not. Where God is directly present, no temple is needed.

Furthermore, the presence of God is so complete that no other light will be necessary: no sun by day, no moon by night (21:23). The old heaven that contained the sun and the moon could be destroyed partly because it was no longer needed. The unmediated glory of God and the Lamb that is the lamp are the sources of light in the new city. This is a further elaboration of 21:3: God will dwell in this new city.

The gates are never closed, which is understandable, both because there is no need for defense and because there is no night, the time when city gates were normally closed. There is no night because the light is the glory of God, and God does not depart from the Holy City.

The Holy City is not the only feature of this new earth. Other nations will be there, but they will look to Jerusalem and bring to it their glory. It is not clear who these other nations are. Evil nations have already been destroyed, as seen in the earlier visions. But at least some members of other nations shall enter it, for their names are written in the Lamb's book of life.

Because the whole city has replaced the Temple, the city is like a temple to the rest of the earth. The people of the city are the priestly people to the whole earth. But who else is on the earth but not in the city? The answer is not clear. Perhaps the redemption of the nations—at least of those whose names are written in the Lamb's book of life— is a process that is not finished with the creation of the new earth. What is clear is that nothing evil, nothing unclean, will be able to contaminate or corrupt the new Jerusalem.

THE NOURISHMENT OF LIFE
Revelation 22:1–5

22:1 **Then the angel showed me the river of the water of life, bright as crystal, flowing from the throne of God and of the Lamb** [2] **through the middle of the street of the city. On either side of the river, is the tree of life with its twelve kinds of fruit, producing its fruit each month; and the leaves of the tree are for the healing of the nations.** [3] **Nothing accursed will be found there any more. But the throne of God and of the Lamb will be in it, and his servants will worship him;** [4] **they will see his face, and his name will be on their foreheads.** [5] **And there will be no more night; they need no light of lamp or sun, for the Lord God will be their light, and they will reign forever and ever.**

The waters of life promised in 21:6 are now pictured as a river flowing from the throne of God and the Lamb, even as the vision of Ezekiel had the river that healed the earth flowing from the new temple (Ezek. 47:1–12). In both Ezekiel's vision and in John's, the imagery goes back to the description of Eden in Genesis 2:9–10, although in these verses it is the tree and not the river that has the name "life" applied to it. In Revelation 22:2, the tree of life is on both sides of the river of life, being nourished by the water.

The concluding chapter of Revelation harks back to the picture of Creation before the Fall. Yet it is not the same. The redemption of the world is not a simple return to the original creation. Eden was not a 1,500 square mile city. All of human history stands in between, complete with the development of civilization, the enormous growth of population, the creation of cities, and all the conflicts of human societies. That is why it is important that John envisions the future as a city, not as a pastoral garden scene, even Eden itself.

The river and the tree of life are now in the midst of the Holy City (22:2). The leaves of the tree of life are to heal the nations. Again, there is a sign of life outside of the city, a life to be healed between the peoples of different nations. The tree of life produces a different fruit each month of the year and therefore gives constant life to those who eat it. Life in the New Jerusalem has characteristics of our earthly life. It is nourished by fruit; there is a seasonality.

The picture given earlier is repeated. Nothing evil will be in this Holy City. The central feature is the throne of God and the Lamb, joined together in the redemptive work. The servants of God and the Lamb will worship, seeing God face-to-face, emphasizing the nearness, the direct presence of God. The redeemed will bear the name of God and the Lamb, even as the condemned bore the mark of the beast. Notice that God and the Lamb are jointly on the throne and jointly worshiped.

WORDS OF AUTHORITY
Revelation 22:6–16

22:6 **And he said to me, "These words are trustworthy and true, for the Lord, the God of the spirits of the prophets, has sent his angel to show his servants what must soon take place."**

[7] **"See, I am coming soon! Blessed is the one who keeps the words of the prophecy of this book."**

[8] **I, John, am the one who heard and saw these things. And when I heard and saw them, I fell down to worship at the feet of the angel who showed them to me;** [9] **but he said to me, "You must not do that! I am a fellow servant with you and your comrades the prophets, and with those who keep the words of this book. Worship God!"**

[10] **And he said to me, "Do not seal up the words of the prophecy of this book, for the time is near.** [11] **Let the evildoer still do evil, and the filthy still be filthy, and the righteous still do right, and the holy still be holy."**

[12] **"See, I am coming soon; my reward is with me, to repay according to everyone's work.** [13] **I am the Alpha and the Omega, the first and the last, the beginning and the end."**

[14] **Blessed are those who wash their robes, so that they will have the right to the tree of life and may enter the city by the gates.** [15] **Outside are the dogs and sorcerers and fornicators and murderers and idolaters, and everyone who loves and practices falsehood.**

[16] **"It is I, Jesus, who sent my angel to you with this testimony for the churches. I am the root and the descendant of David, the bright morning star."**

Several pronouns in this section are somewhat ambiguous. In 22:6 and 22:10 the "he" who speaks may be the angel who has shown John the city.

In 22:6 he announces the validity of the words given to John to proclaim. But in 22:7 the "I" is Jesus speaking in the first person. He announces the closeness of the end time, when he will come again. He then gives a blessing to those who are faithful to the vision given to John.

With these words directly from Jesus, the reader is returned to the atmosphere of the beginning of the book. It was Jesus who commanded John to write the book to be sent to the seven churches. Now that the vision is complete, Jesus blesses those who remain faithful to it. John then adds his own witness that he has indeed written what he saw and heard.

As in 19:10, when the angel assures John of the trustworthiness of what he has been told, John falls to the feet of the angel to worship him, only to be told not to do so. God only is to be worshiped. The angel and John are fellow servants, along with all those who are prophets and with the faithful. John's response shows the overwhelming authority given to the true Word of God. The angel's response shows that the authority given to the Word must not be transferred to the messenger.

It is the angel who tells John not to seal the book that he has written (22:10). This is unlike the visions of Daniel, who was told to seal up his writings, because the time had not yet come for the events depicted in his vision to happen (Dan. 8:26). This is also in contrast to the earlier portion of John's vision, where the book sealed with seven seals could be opened only by the Lamb (5:1–9). That earlier book contained the goal of God's creation and the process by which it would be achieved in history. That goal had been there all the time, but only "the Lamb who was slaughtered" (5:12) could open the sealed scroll after the work of redemption had been accomplished on the cross.

John's vision does refer to future times, but his message clearly is for the Christians of his own day, urging them to remain faithful. It has no need to be sealed. Its time has come, even as the vision is being received.

John knows that he lives in the time before the fulfillment of what he has been shown in his vision. Therefore, it is a time of choice for all people. Those who are evil will still be evil. There will be no apparent penalty for their sinfulness. In fact, given what is said earlier about Babylon, those who are evil may well prosper in the immediate days ahead. Those who are holy should remain holy, even if doing so leads to trouble for them. The end has not yet come. Babylon still depicts the condition in which the earth lives. But John has been given a glimpse of what lies ahead, what even now is being prepared behind the scene. The time is near when his vision will become reality. The present is the time for faithfulness.

The call to faithfulness brings again the words of Jesus, saying that he is coming soon. It is not clear how much of 22:12–16 is to be understood as the words of Jesus. Some commentators put all five verses as a direct quotation. Other assume verses 14 and 15 are the words of the angel spoken between words of Jesus. The meaning remains the same.

As the book draws to a close, the words of Jesus become a blessing or a condemnation for the future readers. Those who are faithful will be able to enter the city of God and eat of the tree of life, which will give them eternal life. Those who are unfaithful will be outside of the city and not receive its blessed inheritance (22:14–15). The words of Jesus reinforce the words of the angel who has led John through the vision (22:16). The angel had been sent by Jesus. It is not John, but the readers, who need this added word of authority.

BACK TO THE LITURGICAL SETTING
Revelation 22:17–21

> 22:17 The Spirit and the bride say, "Come."
> And let everyone who hears say, "Come."
> And let everyone who is thirsty come.
> Let anyone who wishes take the water of life as a gift.
> [18] I warn everyone who hears the words of the prophecy of this book: if anyone adds to them, God will add to that person the plagues described in this book; [19] if anyone takes away from the words of the book of this prophecy, God will take away that person's share in the tree of life and in the holy city, which are described in this book.
> [20] The one who testifies to these things says, "Surely I am coming soon." Amen. Come, Lord Jesus!
> [21] The grace of the Lord Jesus be with all the saints. Amen.

This final section of Revelation is not only an ending; it is also a beginning. There is an invitation issued by the Spirit and the bride. The invitation is to come to take the water of life. The concluding verses make it clear that the invitation is the same as, or at least includes, an invitation to the Lord's table.

These last verses include words that from other sources we know are the liturgical lead into the Eucharist: "Come, Lord Jesus!" These words can be found in the *Didache*, a very early document of church worship. Paul also concludes his first letter to the Corinthians in the same way (1 Cor. 16:22). Paul and the *Didache* use the Aramaic phrase "Maranatha," which in Revelation is put into Greek. Both are translated into English as

"Come, Lord Jesus!" In both Paul and Revelation, the phrase clarifies where such letters were to be read in the worship service.

John's vision was not written to be circulated privately to individual Christians. It was a message to churches and therefore was expected to be read in the gathered community. Its placement in the service is seen in the concluding words. It was an authoritative message to the congregation by one of its own prophets. Remember, John's vision took place on the Lord's day (1:10). Separated from his church, he carries on the role of a prophet in the congregation. He does it in writing when he cannot do it in person. Even the words of blessing and condemnation in 22:14–15 can be understood in this context, as the proper warning to the faithless before the sacrament.

The faithful congregation gathered at the Lord's Table cries to the Lord to be present with them but also to return in the final time with the promised kingdom—in Revelation, the promised city. In the Holy City at the end, the faithful will eat of the tree of life and receive the water of life. Here, the faithful gather at the Table and receive the sacrament as the temporary form of that final eating and drinking. Through the Lord's Table, the faithful are nourished as the bride of the Lamb, being prepared for the marriage feast yet to come. The blessing of 22:21 is also part of the traditional opening of the eucharistic service.

Between the invitation (22:17) and the conclusion (22:20–21) is the final warning to take seriously what John has written. Who is the "I" who says these words (22:18–19)? Most likely it is John himself. This parallels the warning given by Jesus in 22:14–15, although there the warning is addressed to those who do not wash their robes rather than to those who change the words of the book.

John has finished his task. He has faithfully recorded what he has seen and heard in his vision. His words have been authenticated both by the angel and by Jesus himself. Now it is up to those who receive the book to follow its guidance. Will the words be so difficult that some readers will be tempted to tone them down and change them, enabling those readers to compromise with the powers that be? Difficult as they are, the words are to remain. Those who would change them would be revealing that they are among the unfaithful, thereby suffering the consequences described in the book.

Is John's message positive or negative? For the faithful, it is a message of hope and encouragement. It presents a vision of the Holy City that will be their reward and therefore gives them strength to continue along the difficult path. For the wavering, John's message presents a clear choice: remain faithful or be condemned. There is no middle way, no compromise with the evil structures that control so much of earthly life. For them, it may be a frightening message, for it shows that life is about to be more difficult for the faithful, rather than easier.

For those whose clear desire is to remain faithful, the final verses of the book point to the reality of Christ's presence in their midst even now, in the form of the sacrament. For all, the promise and the warning have been given. It is up to the reader, the hearer of John's vision to respond to the invitation.

Works Cited

Boring, M. Eugene. *Revelation*. Interpretation. Louisville, Ky.: Westminster John Knox Press, 1989.

Conn, Robert H. *Revelation*. Basic Bible Commentary. Nashville: Abingdon Press, 1988.

Ford, J. Massingberde. *Revelation*. The Anchor Bible. New York: Doubleday, 1975.

Harrington, Wilfrid J. *Revelation*. Sacra Pagina. Collegeville, Minn.: Liturgical Press, 1993.

Rogers, Cornish R. and Josephe R. Jeter, eds., *Preaching through the Apocalypse*. St. Louis: Chalice Press, 1992.

Roloff, Jürgen. *Revelation: A Continental Commentary*. Minneapolis: Fortress Press, 1993.

The hymn "Holy, Holy, Holy! Lord God Almighty!" is written by Reginald Heber and is found in the *Presbyterian Hymnal*, no. 138. Louisville, Ky.: Westmister/John Knox Press, 1990.

Please note that the following abbreviations are also used throughout the text:

KJV, *King James Version* (Nashville, Tenn.: Thomas Nelson Inc., Publisher, 1982).

NIV, *New International Version* (Grand Rapids, Mich.: Zondervan Bible Publishers, 1984).